This Book Is For

All Adult Curioso

Seekers For Their

Personal Collections And

Enjoyment In Adult

Reading

ABOVE: *The inside front cover*
copy from Nights of Horror.

SECRET IDENTITY

SECRET IDENTITY

THE FETISH ART OF
SUPERMAN'S
CO-CREATOR
JOE SHUSTER

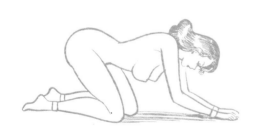

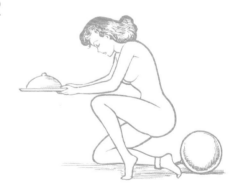

CRAIG YOE

INTRODUCTION BY
STAN LEE

ABRAMS COMICARTS
NEW YORK

This book is dedicated to

The Hero Initiative,
which provides a financial safety net to comic book creators in need.
www.heroinitiative.org

The Comic Book Legal Defense Fund,
which defends the comics industry's First Amendment rights.
www.cbldf.org

The International Team of Comics Historians (ITCH),
which researches and propagates the rich history of cartoonists.
www.superitch.com

Thanks to the following people who did such a spanking good job helping me whip this book into shape:

Much primary research was done on this book. I got terrific, enthusiastic help from the extraordinary Warren Bernard. I interviewed journalist Judith Crist, who originally reported on these historical events; Joe Shuster's friend and fellow cartoonist Jerry Robinson; Dick Ayers, who worked with Joe on *Funnyman;* cartoonist Gill Fox, a great admirer of Shuster; Eugene Maletta, the printer of *Nights of Horror;* cartoonist Gene Basset, who was a courtroom artist for the *Brooklyn Eagle* during the Brooklyn Thrill Killers trial; Bob Weber, a contemporary of Shuster at the Humorama publications; and Boody Rogers, the subject of my book *Boody: The Bizarre Comics of Boody Rogers.* Deep gratitude to all the above for giving me their valuable time and insight.

I deeply appreciate Stan Lee who, if not Superman, certainly is The Man! (Stan, I promise you a walk-on part when they make the movie.)

Clizia Gussoni is always there for me, being encouraging, loyal, and loving—and was an astute copy editor and designer. Our fellow workers at YOE! Studio did a wonderful job, especially Jayne Antipow as senior project manager; Mike Hill as phenomenal production designer; Luke McDonnell and Priya Rajdev, who helped tremendously in the early stage; and Susan Hack-Lane, our in-house publicist. David Burd was a constant wise muse. Bradley Ricca shared invaluable knowledge. Jeff Trexler lent much welcomed research help.

At Abrams, Charlie Kochman's ideas, enthusiasm, and guidance were immeasurable—Charlie was a dream editor. Many thanks also to Eric Himmel, Sofia Gutiérrez, and Andrea Colvin.

Fellow historians generously shared ideas. Many thanks to Jon Anderson, Ron Antonucci, Lucy Caswell, Gregory DeWolfe, Sara Duke, Ron Goulart, Mark Newgarden, Marc Nobleman, Jenny Robb, Charlie Roberts, J. B. Rund, and C. J. Scheiner. And a very special thank you to Bill Blackbeard!

A grateful acknowledgment to the Cleveland Public Library, the Kinsey Institute, the Library of Congress, the National Archives, the New York City Hall Library, the Ohio State University Cartoon Research Library, the Peekskill Public Library, and the San Francisco Academy of Comic Art.

Image Credits: page 9 (top) Cleveland Public Library; page 14 (top) Jerry Robinson; page 14, (bottom) Jeff Delaney; page 16, Vince Oliva; page 17, Bud Plant and Steve Adamovich; page 22, Bill Janocha; page 23 (bottom) Bradley Ricca; pages 24 (top) and 26, The National Archives; page 27, Frank Motler; page 28, Jim Vadeboncoeur, Jr., The Vadeboncoeur Collection of Images; pages 30, 32, and 33, The National Archives. Superman copyright © DC Comics.

Unless noted above, all images shown in this book are from my personal collection. The spot illustrations are from *Continental* magazine.

—CY, 2008

Web site: www.yoe.com/blog: www.superitch.com/e-mail: yoecomix@hotmail.com

Editor: Charles Kochman
Editorial Assistant: Sofia Gutiérrez
Designer: Craig Yoe/YOE! Studio
Production Manager: Alison Gervais

Library of Congress Control Number: 2008934533
Text and compilation copyright © 2009 Craig Yoe
Introduction copyright © 2009 Stan Lee

HNA ▮▮▮▮▮
harry n. abrams, inc.
a subsidiary of La Martinière Groupe
115 West 18th Street
New York, NY 10011
www.hnabooks.com

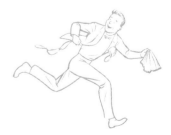

INTRODUCTION STAN LEE

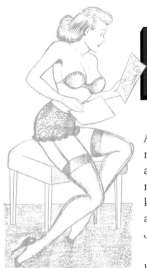

Although I'm a guy who's lived with heroes, most of them were fictitious. But Jerry Siegel and Joe Shuster are right at the top of my list of real-life heroes. While I was lucky enough to know Jerry—in fact he worked at my bullpen for a while—I regret to say that I never actually met Joe. That was my loss.

For anyone who's from another planet and unaware of this culturally potent fact, Joe Shuster was the artist who gave us the very first two-fisted comic book crimefighter in a cape and leotard. Man, that was some departure from all the other drawings of heroes I or anyone else had ever seen. Joe took a concept that had been in Jerry's mind and depicted it in his own simplistic yet highly dramatic style.

It's no secret that Superman was the first of all costumed comic book super heroes and, even today, his image is probably the first that comes to mind when thinking of the phrase "super hero." It's hard to believe that Joe Shuster first drew the man from Krypton's famous alter ego three quarters of a century ago, because that image is still one of the most recognizable in the world.

One of the ironies of life is the fact that in comic book stories the good guy always wins out, and yet in real life neither Jerry nor Joe reaped any vast financial rewards from their creation. In fact, Joe Shuster eventually found himself in a position where he had to accept any art job that was offered to him because of his need for funds. And that brings us to Craig Yoe and the subject of this book.

My colorful friend Craig is an amazing historian who always manages to pull fantastic cultural discoveries out of his propeller beanie hat. It was he who unearthed the unusual material in this offbeat and somewhat startling book. How he found it I'll never know, but it clearly indicates how desperate Joe must have been to have participated in such a project.

Obviously, there's far more sexy stuff here within these pages than you'll find in any mainstream super hero comic book. Much of it isn't the sort of material that rings my bell, but it certainly gives us a clue to what must have been Joe's frame of mind and the state of his morale at that time. Whereas everything about the stories and artwork of Superman was positive and morally uplifting, the pages of *Nights of Horror* that appear in *Secret Identity* cater to the basest of man's character and morals.

This book lays bare the dramatic story of an enthusiastic, perhaps even inspired, artist who gave the reading public one of its greatest icons, only to become so disillusioned and desperate that he was later forced to accept commissions to draw what amounted to S&M erotic horror books, material that was the diametric opposite of the type of heroic adventure with which he had hoped to make his living—and for which he will ever be known.

The entire story of Joe Shuster, one replete with drama and tragedy, is a tale that has never before been revealed in such a graphic and uncensored manner. Some of the material in the book may seem shocking; some figured strongly in censorship investigations in Congress; but all of it will certainly give you pause as you consider the consequences that can ensue when a gifted man is forced to lend his talent to the most sordid of projects.

Excelsior!

SECRET IDENTITY

CRAIG YOE

Superman was an authentic American dream; he simply outclassed all rivals and seemed to thrive on having enemies. Indeed—the dark side of the myth—he seemed to almost generate them.

—Dennis Dooley, *Superman at Fifty* (1988)

Two nerdy teenage Jewish boys from Cleveland create Superman, the Man of Steel.

Two nerdy teenage Jewish boys from Brooklyn kill while on a "supreme adventure" and end up behind iron bars.

How these boys are connected amazingly involves evil mobsters; panting sado-masochists; pervy pornographers; blue-nosed censors; a rabid shrink; a pious minister; a slimy publisher; good cops; bad cops; sexy showgirls; book-burning Supreme Court judges; a pretty artist's model; a poetry-spouting, songwriting defense lawyer; a hell-bent, coonskin-capped senator; horse-whipped girls; murdered bums; and neo-Nazi, Jewish, juvenile delinquents known as the Brooklyn Thrill Killers.

As the Superman comics used to say: "Not a dream! Not a hoax! Not an imaginary story!"

Like his character, Joseph Shuster the artist, co-creator of Superman, had a Ma and Pa Kent, a Clark Kent, and a Lois Lane in his life.

"Ma and Pa Kent" were, of course, his mom and dad, who kindly encouraged his artistic pursuits. Mamma Shuster brought home brown wrapping paper from the butcher for the young Joe to draw on. Papa Shuster brought home the *Cleveland Plain Dealer,* from which Joe copied his favorite Sunday funnies.

"Clark Kent" was a geeky science fiction fan and writer, Jerry Siegel, Joe's best pal since they were sixteen.

For the role of "Lois Lane," there were at least two candidates in Joe's life. In an interview in the *Washington Star* in 1975, Joe confided that he "had a crush" on a Lois Amster. "She's a grandmother now in Cleveland, but I don't think she has any idea that she was the inspiration for Lois Lane."

The other "Lois" was a dark-haired teen named Jolan Kovacs. She entered Joe's life when she placed an ad in the *Plain Dealer,* wanting to become an artist's model. Joe was happy to draw her in his bedroom, as she wore her sister's baggy swimsuit. Now and then his mother checked in, while the girl's mother waited downstairs. Jolan became the original model for Superman's Lois Lane. Jolan and Joe had a few Pop's Soda Shoppe–type dates, and kept in touch the rest of their lives.

Although not from the planet Krypton, Joe Shuster was an alien of sorts. He was from Toronto, Canada, born there on July 10, 1914. At ten years old, Joe found himself on the U.S. side of Lake Erie, in Cleveland, Ohio. His father, Julius, and his mother, Ida, moved Joe, his

SUPERMAN

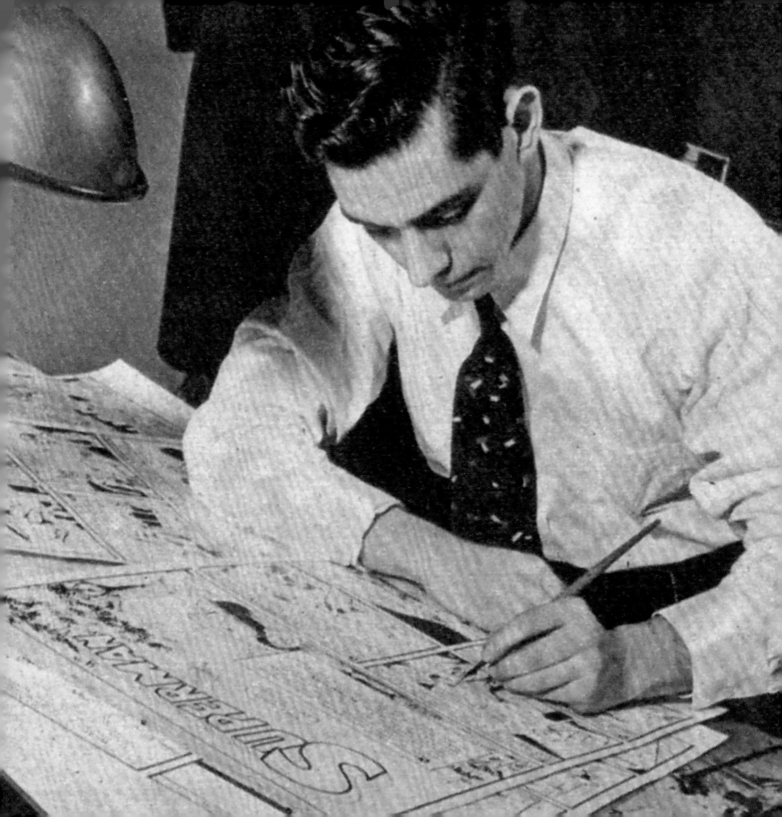

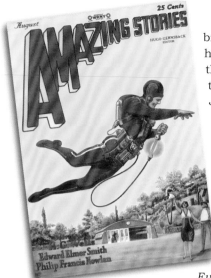

brother, Frank, and his sister, Jean, there to partake of the American Way. Joe's grandparents were Russian and his father came to Canada via Holland.

Joe Shuster was a short, thin, "pale, pitcher-eared lad," according to the *Saturday Evening Post.* By Joe's own admission, he was "mild-mannered, wore glasses, was very shy around women." Joe was a "before" in the comic strip bodybuilding ads of Charles Atlas, "the world's most perfect man." The "before" who might get sand kicked in his face at the beach. A July 1946 *Coronet* article states, "Superman is the by-product of the frustrated boyhood of two undersized Cleveland youths, Jerry Siegel and Joe Shuster. While high school students, the duo absorbed beatings from neighborhood toughs."

The Shuster family lived in a tiny apartment, in a poor section of Cleveland called Glenville, on the corner of Armor and Parkwood. The Shusters routinely had a tough time scrapping together the twenty-dollar-a-month rent. Some nights the family was forced to endure involuntary fasting.

When there were regular meals, they were often put on the table thanks to Joe. The young Shuster sold newspapers or ice cream cones to supplement his father's meager earnings as an occasional tailor. It wouldn't be the last time Joe helped support his family.

After supper, Joe would clean up the table, then hurry to his bedroom. There the neophyte artist would take out a stubby, yellow pencil and butcher-shop brown paper, and escape into the world of drawing cartoons. During cold Cleveland winters, bitter chills came off Lake Erie. When the family had no coal to burn, Joe had to wear gloves, two or three sweaters, and sometimes more than one jacket while he was drawing his pictures.

His sketches resembled the comic strip characters of the day, including Popeye, the humorous, superstrong, one-eyed, two-fisted sailor; the more adventure-styled Wash Tubbs; and the fantastic Little Nemo. Buck Rogers, Flash Gordon, and Tarzan rocketed and swung by a little later.

After classes, Joe went to the newsstand to soak up more fantastical visuals from pulp magazines. During these Great Depression years, he couldn't afford the dime admission price to the pulps. So the youthful artist memorized ideas from the lurid, bombastic covers, which he stored in his memory bank. At fourteen, Shuster furtively spied the August 1928 issue of the science fiction pulp *Amazing Stories.* It sported a bold painting by Frank R. Paul of a flying man in a skintight red suit being admired by a woman below. This evocative scene caused Joe's imagination to soar to new heights. Shuster told comic historian Shel Dorf, "What I considered the best inspiration was seeing the work of artists like MiltonCaniff, Alexander Raymond, and well-known science fiction artist Frank R. Paul."

A young writer of Joe's age and from his neighborhood was Jerome Siegel. Jerry independently saw the same issue of *Amazing Stories.* The inside of the magazine contained the first Buck Rogers story in prose form, but it was the cover more than anything that created in the young teenagers a sense of wonder. Doc Savage was another pulp hero who stoked the boys' creativity. Savage's first name was Clark; he had an Arctic Fortress of Solitude; and he was boldly heralded an

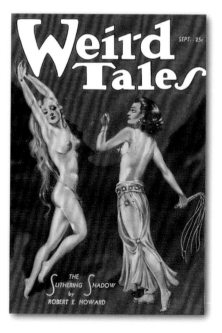

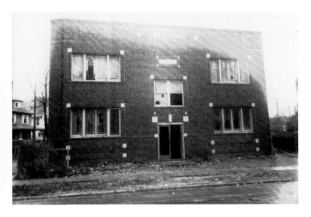

all-caps "SUPER-MAN" in ads touting his adventures. Savage was one of a number of pulp protagonists at the time referred to as Superman. Author Philip Wylie's *Gladiator* (1930), about a biologist who turned his son into an "invulnerable man," was undoubtedly another influence helping spawn Siegel and Shuster's Superman. Golden Age artist Boody Rogers called the *Gladiator*'s effect on Jerry and Joe, "Hell, the whole inspiration!"

Siegel and Shuster met at Glenville High, as members of the staff of the *Glenville Torch.* They soon concocted a hand-typed fanzine, a poor man's pulp, simply called *Science Fiction,* printing it on the school's mimeograph machine. The third issue, brought out in January 1933, contained a story, *The Reign of the Super-Man,* with the protagonist portrayed as a villain.

Joe didn't sign the art on this Super-Man, though it's unmistakably his, and Jerry used the pen name Herbert S. Fine, who was his cousin. An ad placed in their high school paper had promised *Science Fiction* would feature "action-adventure stories upon this and other worlds by several prominent Glenvilites writing under pseudonyms." In 1934, discussing features created for the *Cleveland Shopping News,* Jerry recalled, "We used pseudonyms on some strips, while others were anonymous. But I wrote every word and Joe did all the artwork himself, including penciling, inking, and lettering."

The work for the *Cleveland Shopping News* didn't pan out, but another idea, which had been incubating, eventually would. Siegel had been working on Superman because, some say, he needed an invulnerable hero after tragically losing his father, who died of a heart attack when his tailor shop was robbed. Jerry had even created sample strips of Superman with cartoonist Russell Keaton. But, as the story goes, one hot summer night in Cleveland, all of Jerry's influences and ideas perfectly crystallized. A blindingly bright cartoon lightbulb lit above his round, boyish head telling him exactly how he would approach Superman with his neighborhood pal Joe Shuster. Jerry scribbled notes through the night, and the next morning quickly threw on his clothes over his pajamas. His coat flapped behind him like a cape as he hurriedly ran over to Joe's house, nearly ten blocks away, and this dynamic duo put their heads together. Joe excitedly pushed his pencil across the paper as Jerry described Superman, now no longer a villain, but a hero!

Joe's pictures of this super crimefighter became worth a thousand words, a million words even, and worth millions and millions of dollars. Joe gave Superman muscles like those he saw in the pages of popular bodybuilding magazines. He festooned the character in a circus-type costume, complete with cape, and an identifying triangle-bordered "S" on his chest. All this was beautifully rendered in Joe's simple, strong, and engaging style, which he distilled from the comics he loved. Taking a lesson from the brightly hued pulp covers of Frank R. Paul, Joe could not have colored Superman's costume more vibrantly, with its primary blue, red, and yellow.

The teen titans were onto something. Buck Rogers and Flash Gordon may have been thrilling because they went to other planets, but Superman trumped them both by *coming* from outer space. And when Superman landed on planet Earth, he adopted possibly the most intriguing aspect of his persona: a *secret identity!* Having a secret identity

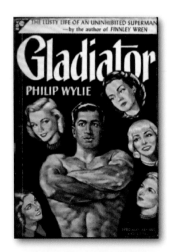

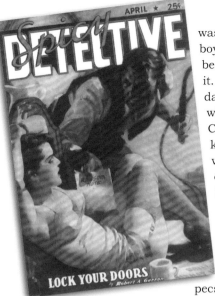

was something the boys knew well—because they lived it. If that desirable dame Lois Lane, who disdained Clark Kent, only knew who he was in reality. If only she knew he was Superman, who lifted cars, punched out villains, bounced bullets off his pecs, bounded over skyscrapers, and even had X-ray vision!

And the girls at Glenville High, if only they knew that the original nerds, Jerry and Joe, had just created the most iconic fictional hero of all time!

Creating Superman was the easy part; selling him was hard. Siegel and Shuster believed in the immigrant from Krypton, but couldn't find a publisher who wanted him to appear in the panels of its comics. After a few false starts, the boys went for the top: the lucrative and prestigious newspaper comic strip syndicates. Over the next few years, they worked their way down to the primitive, pulpy, and fledging world of newsstand comic books.

Jerry and Joe had been creating adventures for this new medium starting in *New Fun*'s sixth issue (October 1935). For this comic, Jerry and Joe conceived Henri Duval of France, Famed Soldier of Fortune, and Doctor Occult, the Ghost Detective, whose tales they signed "Leger and Reuths." *New Fun* became *More Fun* in 1936, where Siegel and Shuster also conceived *Calling All Cars,* which later became *Radio Squad,* featuring Sandy Kean.

Federal Men joined this menagerie of crimefighters in *New Comics* no. 2 (January 1936). In the same issue, Siegel and Shuster introduced a two-fisted detective named Slam Bradley, a precursor of Superman. Finally their publisher, National (later called DC Comics), had some space to fill in a book about to launch called *Action Comics.* The editor took a flying leap in publishing this blue union-suited, bullet-bouncing, train-outrunning muscle man with a handsome forehead spit curl—Superman!

The publisher of Superman was Harry Donenfeld. Donenfeld liked to brag that he was friends with high-level mobsters like Frank Costello. Before National, Donenfeld got his start printing pornography in the twenties and thirties. His fare was photo magazines with titles like *Modern Art* and *French Art and Models.* These periodicals, purportedly for "art students," reprinted blown-up French postcards of Paris prostitutes, and featured pictures of New York showgirls sans costumes. Harry's more prose-oriented publications brandished titles like *Spicy Stories, Juicy Tales, Hot Stories, La Paree Stories,* and *Gay Parisienne,* mostly sold under the counter. The covers sported sex-charged pin-ups that lured in the horny readers. The libidinous paintings were by gifted pulp artists like Enoch Bolles and H. J. Ward. Later, Ward did a six-foot portrait of Superman for the DC boardroom after the Man from Krypton filled Harry Donenfeld's coffers.

Harry Donenfeld also published a traditional pulp magazine, interestingly titled *Super-Detective.* But the publisher hit on the idea for cranking up the

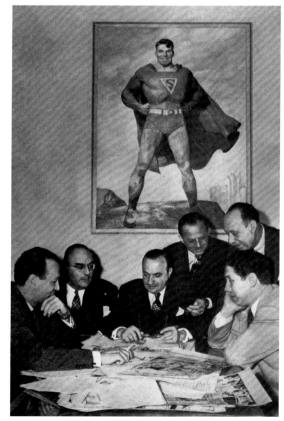

volume by combining the detective genre with the risqué magazine shtick. *Spicy Detective,* then *Spicy Mystery, Spicy Western,* and *Spicy Adventure,* immediately joined *Super-Detective.* The sugar and spice and everything naughty covers featured girl detectives with ripped clothing wrestling girl mobsters; half-naked girls bound and gagged; and satanic villains flogging scantily clad girls.

Girls, girls, girls, sex, sex, sex, violence, violence, violence!

Harry's sizzling success with his salacious magazines created both competitors and critics. Anthony Comstock's New York Society for the Suppression of Vice came down on him. The National Organization for Decent Literature described the spicy pulps as "wholly depraved and lascivious, and undoubtedly one of the deadliest plagues that ever threatened the moral life of a nation."

In contrast, Superman stood for—and leaped tall buildings for—all that was good: Truth, Justice, and the American Way! Siegel proclaimed that Superman had the "morals of Sir Galahad." Science fiction author Harlan Ellison writes, "He is more than the fanciful daydream of two Cleveland schoolboys. He is the twentieth-century archetype of mankind at its finest. He is courage and humanity, steadfastness and decency, responsibility and ethic. He is our universal longing for perfection, for wisdom and power used in the service of the human race."

By the time the idea and the ideal finally sold,

Jerry and Joe weren't teenagers but in their twenties, and were thrilled to see their creation in print at last. The gifted team had gathered only reject letters, one of which deemed their champion "too fantastic." Donenfeld paid the not-so-fantastic sum of $130 for the thirteen-page origin story, and bought out all rights to Superman. The Man of Tomorrow debuted in *Action Comics* no.1 (June 1938).

Shuster's artwork was as dynamic as the hero himself. Playwright and cartoonist Jules Feiffer opined in 1965 that Joe's "work was direct, unprettied—crude and vigorous; as easy to read as a diagram. No creamy lines, no glossy effects, no touch of that bloodless prefabrication that passes for professionalism these days." And *these* days.

Joe anticipated success and the inability to keep up with the resulting workload. In addition, his work was painstaking due to the weak eyes that plagued him his whole life. Shuster began placing classified ads in *Professional Art Quarterly,* starting with the Summer 1938 issue. This call for help appeared on the newsstands at the same time as Superman's debut. The ad read, "HELP WANTED. ARTIST with ability to draw action-adventure strips; assist on nationally established features; send samples. Joseph E. Shuster, 10905 Amor Ave., Cleveland, Ohio."

The story in the first issue of *Action Comics* closed with a prediction. Years later Jerry Siegel said, "You'll note that in the very last panel we say, 'And so begins the startling adventures of the most sensational strip character of all time.' And that may sound a little conceited but that's the way we felt about the character." Jerry and Joe's longtime faith in Superman had been well-founded. In a development quite uncharacteristic for a comic book, newsdealers called for more copies of *Action Comics* right after it hit the stands. By the seventh issue, DC was moving half a

RIGHT: *Joe's classified ad calling for help in* Professional Art Quarterly *(Summer 1938).*

BELOW: *The Creatives. Pencilled on the back of this 1940 photo are these notes: "Editorial conference: (left to right) Ed Dubrotka, inker; Wayne Boring, syndication; Joe Shuster, art director; Jerry Siegel, idea man; Frank Shuster, letterer and Joe's kid brother; Leo Nowak, penciller." A rubber stamp reveals, "Photo by Dork."*

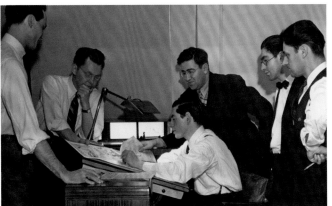

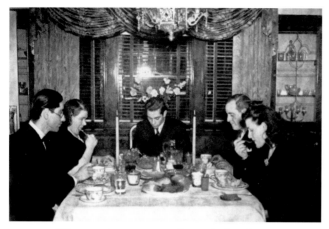

million copies per month, and that figure quickly almost doubled.

Superman soon boasted his own self-titled comic book, displayed alongside *Action*. It sold even better than its predecessor. The Man of Steel spawned a whole industry and hundreds of super characters to populate it: from Amazing-Man to Zatara. It was a wonder that, with this army of super crimefighters, there was any criminal activity left in the world at all!

If publishers had been slow to recognize the power and worth of Superman, the *kids* immediately got it. Superman pried a lot of dimes out of their little fists. Supermania reigned. In addition to buying the comics, the kids flocked to the Superman movie serials, religiously tuned in to his radio and television adventures, and flew around in their backyards wearing pint-sized Superman costumes.

The disparity of what Siegel and Shuster earned and what Donenfeld raked in from Superman's success greatly annoyed Jerry and Joe. They were, however, paternalistically thrown a big bone on the newspaper syndication deal. Superman finally burst into the Fourth Estate funnies through the back door. The McClure Syndicate, which had previously turned Supes down, could no longer deny the superstar's appeal. According to different reports, Jerry and Joe received anywhere from 50 to 90 percent of the considerable proceeds of the Superman newspaper strip.

Superman's comic strips started in just four newspapers in January 1939, but quickly grew

to appear in over three hundred daily and ninety Sunday papers. Over 20,000,000 readers devoured it. The 1942 book *Comics and Their Creators* leads off the section on Superman with: "Many a youngster gifted enough to scrawl the caricature of teacher on the blackboard dreams of becoming a famous cartoonist with a two-yacht income and a short working day. Such windfalls used to occur only in the comics. But the real life story of two Cleveland, Ohio, youths, Jerry Siegel and Joe Shuster, parallels the Number One daydream of American youth. Their brainchild, which pays each of them in the neighborhood of fifty thousand dollars a year [equivalent to $750,000 today], is Superman, the one-man brawn trust of the adventure strips."

On June 21, 1941, the *Saturday Evening Post* featured an expansive article about the popularity of Superman and the fortunes of Joe, Jerry, and their publisher. A caption under a photo of Joe's family in their plush home said, "None of the Shusters can quite grasp what has happened to them. Joe is a bountiful provider for Brother Frank, Mamma, Papa, and Sister Jeanette." The *Post* described Shuster as a "good provider for his whole family," and spoke of their new, ten-room wooden frame house as being in a "better neighborhood . . . and filled with shiny new furniture, including a sixteen-tube radio phonograph console, so that Joe and Mamma Shuster can share their favorite pastime—listening to classical music." The artist "has also bought a fancy automobile, shelves of detective stories, and a camera." The periodical revealed, "But Mamma Shuster still waits on the table, the only concession to her improved status being a colored maid, who comes in twice a week to house-clean."

The article went on to illustrate two sides of Shuster who, though now well-off, liked to dress scruffily. It is poignant because it foretells a post-Superman anecdote about a destitute Shuster. "Last December [1940] in Miami Beach, where he liked to loiter hatless and in shabby clothes along uppity Lincoln Road, gawking at

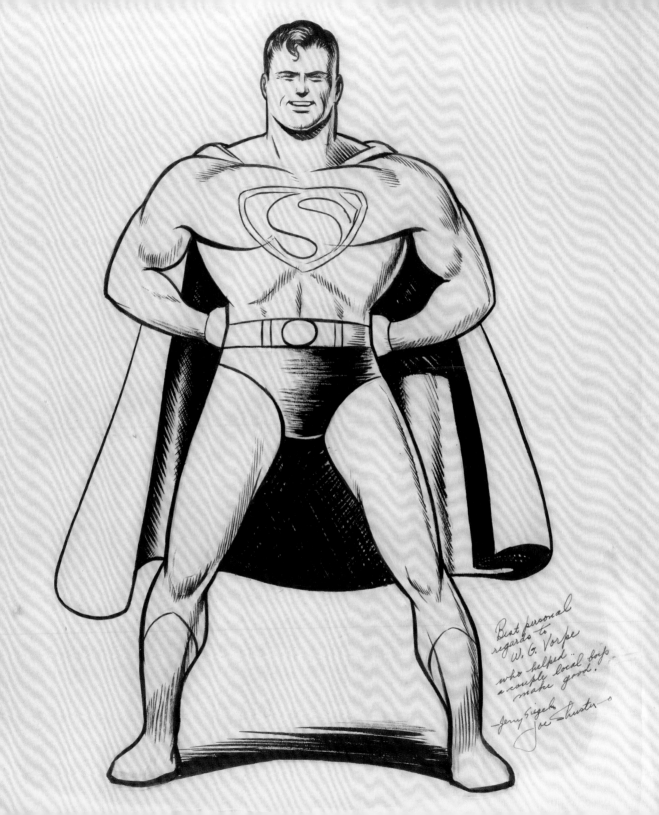

Best personal
regards to
W. G. Vorpe
who helped
a couple local boys
make good.
Jerry Siegel
Joe Shuster

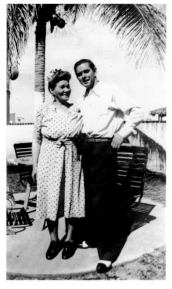

expensive automobiles, a policeman approached Shuster, bristling with dark suspicions. Probably nothing would have happened had Shuster not protested that he was Superman's co-creator and flashed $147 in large bills to show he was no derelict. The policeman arrested him, and a magistrate sentenced him to thirty days in the pen for vagrancy. A local reporter had the wit to suggest that Shuster establish his identity by drawing Superman. Face crimson, the court let him go." This wouldn't be the only time Shuster and Superman would be found in court, and the story would not always have an upbeat ending.

You couldn't judge Superman by his first cover. The front of *Action Comics* no. 1 depicted the protagonist lifting a car above his head and smashing it against a rock as people ran for shelter, their eyes bugging out and sweat leaping from their brows in the best cartoon tradition. Was Superman good or bad? We learn inside that the Man of Steel was good, but some critics never saw him and his cronies that way.

Children's book author Sterling North blasted comics in the *Chicago Daily News* (May 8, 1940), headlined "A National Disgrace." "Virtually every child in America is reading color 'comic' magazines—a poisonous mushroom growth of the last two years. Ten million copies of these sex-horror serials are sold every month. The bulk of these lurid publications depends for their appeal upon mayhem, murder, torture and abduction, Superman heroics, voluptuous females in scanty attire found on almost every page. Badly drawn, badly written, and badly printed, the effect of these pulp-paper night-mares is that of a violent stimulant."

In a follow-up article entitled "The Antidote to Comics," for the National Parent-Teacher Association in March 1941, North offered his moral compass: "The chances of Fascism controlling the planet diminish in direct proportion to the number of good books the coming generation reads and enjoys."

In the February 1943 issue of *Catholic World,* Reverend Thomas Doyle wrote a rhetorically titled article, "What's Wrong with the Comics?" The Reverend said that Superman "in a vulgar way seems to personify the primitive religion expounded by Nietzsche's *Zarathustra.* 'Man alone is and must be our God,' says Zarathustra, very much in the style of a Nazi pamphleteer."

Dr. Paul A. Witty, professor of education at Northwestern University, declared that the super hero comics "present our world in a kind of Fascist setting of violence and hate and destruction. The democratic ideals that we should seek are likely to be overlooked."

Dr. Fredric Wertham, a noted psychiatrist who often dealt with children and the subject of violence, echoed these criticisms of Superman. Wertham's 1953 *Seduction of the Innocent,* a highly influential, anti-comics, book-length discourse, declared, "We established the basic ingredients of the most numerous and widely read

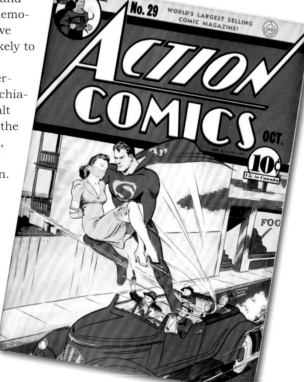

LEFT: *Joe's friend, cartoonist Jerry Robinson, took this photo of Joe and his mother in Miami, in the early 1940s.*

BELOW: *Superman rescues Lois Lane after she has been bound and gagged by mobsters on the cover of* Action Comics no. 29 (October 1940). *In the upper left of the cover, Superman is breaking a chain with his pecs. Bondage? Superman was against it!*

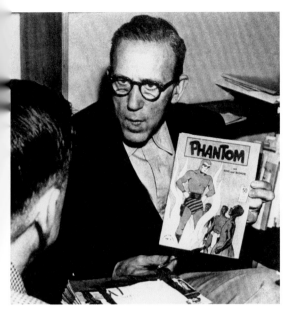

ABOVE: *Dr. Fredric Wertham thought super heroes were fascist, and white jungle lord comics characters were racist. He was not a big* Phantom *fan.*

comic books: violence, sadism, and cruelty; the superman philosophy, an offshoot of Nietzsche's superman, who said, 'When you go to women, don't forget the whip.'"

Wertham went on to say, "The supermen are either half undressed or dressed in fancy raiment that is a mixture of the costumes of SS men, divers, and robots. In one comic book of the group, old-fashioned mugging—in recent years so frequently practiced by juveniles in large cities—is a recurrent theme. Blood flows freely, bosoms are half bared, girls' buttocks are drawn with careful attention."

Wertham contended that Superman caused troubled children to have "fantasies of sadistic joy in seeing other people punished over and over while you yourself remain immune." The psychiatrist deemed this the "Superman Complex."

Gershon Legman, author of the first book on oral sex and who claimed to have coined the phrase "Make love not war" in the '60s, wrote in 1949, "In the hands of the Supermen, private justice takes over. No trial is necessary, no stupid policemen hog all the fun. Fists crashing into faces become the court of highest appeal. The truth is that the Superman formula is, in every particular, the exact opposite of what it pretends to be.

"The Superman virus was sown, not, of course by the two nice Jewish boys who take the credit, Messrs. Shuster and Siegel, but by Hitler. With only this difference that, in the ten-year effort to keep supplying sinister victims for the Supermen to destroy, comic-books have succeeded in giving every American child a complete course in paranoid megalomania such as no

German child ever had, a total conviction of the morality of force such as no Nazi could ever aspire to."

Besides the alleged fascism of Superman, Dr. Fredric Wertham was concerned by the sexual message comic books telescoped to young readers. *Seduction of the Innocent* warned, "The keynote of the comic books' sexual message, drummed into children from a tender age on, is the admixture of sensuality with cruelty. The illustrations are, as the *Art Digest* called them, 'perverted.' It is a special perversion that they cultivate most of all, sadism. Sadism is defined as 'the gratification of sexual feeling by the infliction of or sight of pain.'"

During all this, it pained Siegel to see Donenfeld get the big bucks as Superman flew higher and higher. When drafted into the army during World War II, Jerry became an editor at the *Stars and Stripes Pacific Edition,* based in Hawaii. There he met a man who could change all that. Aloha, Albert Zugsmith! Zugsmith was a journalist, a player in the entertainment world of New York, and a part-time lawyer. Jerry and Albert became friends and, after the war, it was Siegel, Shuster, and Zugsmith vs. Donenfeld, the Man of Steal.

There was a full-scale war going on now against comic books by psychiatrists, senators, religious leaders, and parent groups. Siegel and Shuster were nearing the end of their ten-year contract. It seemed like a needful time to attempt to void their original contract, which granted DC ownership of Superman, so they sued and petitioned the court for five million dollars in damages. They also brought a claim for the rights to Superboy, which they contended was Jerry's idea. The trial was held in White Plains, New York, a half hour from New York City, and ten minutes from the beautiful Hudson River.

The trial ended in 1948 and, when Justice J. Addison Young handed down the ruling, it was disappointing. Jerry and Joe were awarded the rights for Superboy, for which DC paid only

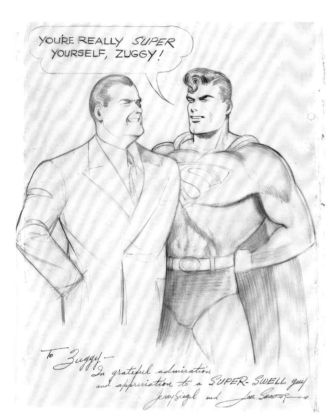

YOU'RE REALLY *SUPER* YOURSELF, ZUGGY!

To Zuggy—
In grateful admiration and appreciation to a SUPER-SWELL guy
Jerry Siegel and Joe Shuster—

LEFT: *Was this drawing presented by Siegel and Shuster to Albert "Zuggy" Zugsmith before or after the 1948 court decision?*

$94,000. Much of the settlement probably went to their lawyer. Albert Zugsmith took his earnings to Hollywood, and produced flicks such as *Dondi* and *Confessions of an Opium Eater.*

But the Biggie, Superman's ownership: The judge upheld DC's position that the $130 paid for Superman's first story made the character a work-for-hire proposition, and was now owned outright by DC.

In *Men of Tomorrow,* Gerard Jones reports that Shuster harbored a lifelong suspicion that "Zuggy" took a kickback from DC, and sold him and Siegel down the Hudson River.

The originators of Superman unceremoniously became personae non gratae at DC Comics. Siegel and Shuster received no more writing and art assignments. Their names were axed from the credits on the comics and not found on any more DC checks. The now powerful publishing house built on the muscled back of Siegel and Shuster's Man of Steel became a Fortress of Ingratitude.

According to his sister Jean, Shuster became depressed. Joe said, "We did not foresee that our creation would be taken away from us, our by-lines stripped from us, and a host of other writers and artists brought in, first to compete with us and then to replace us. We still find it hard to comprehend how it is possible that we, the creators of what has been called 'one of the most phenomenal success stories of the twentieth century,' have been totally and completely deprived and divested of our work by a web of legal technicalities, and then abandoned."

Jerry Robinson, the creator of Batman's villain the Joker, was Joe's friend. For *Secret Identity,* Robinson shared what losing the litigation meant for Shuster. Robinson's story parallels the Miami Beach incident, when Shuster was run in by a cop, this time without the happy ending. "Once Joe had lost the court case, he was despairing. Joe told me this story himself. He was picked up by a cop on a bench in Central Park, as a vagrant and hungry. The cop bought him a sandwich in a local luncheonette. Joe saw some kids looking at comics, and so, to prove who he was, drew a picture of Superman. I don't know if they ever believed him, but he did it. It was sad."

Before the suit, Siegel and Shuster realized that they were risking the loss of their incomes from DC. As a backup plan, they came up with another super hero, Funnyman. While Superman's suit was inspired by the strong men of the circus, Funnyman's costume came from the clowns. In 1948, they sold the concept as a comic book to Magazine Enterprises (ME) and as a strip to the Bell Syndicate. Jerry and Joe had great hopes for their humorous hero. Along with Ernie Bache and Marvin Stein, Joe drafted Dick Ayers, in his professional debut, to work on the new character. "Joe seldom came into work," Ayers explained. "He would just on occasion come into the Manhattan studio and supervised as much as he could. Joe came and looked. He would hold up the drawing close to his face so he could see it. He had very thick glasses. Joe would take a little scrap of paper and draw me the mouth or the hands the way he wanted them. It was little intricate things like those that he caught."

Joe liked Ayers's work on the *Funnyman* comic books, and asked him to work on the strip. But Joe was running out of money. Ayers reports, "I only did about three weeks of strips, I think, because Joe couldn't pay. You always had to kind of drag it out of him. It didn't seem as though Jerry and Joe had anything."

The jokes in *Funnyman* fell flat, and Siegel and Shuster were close to being flat broke. *Funnyman* lasted only six issues, and the strip ended soon after the comic book's demise.

Jerry was able to find work as a writer and editor. He was hired for a large salary at Ziff-Davis, and then at Famous Funnies, in hopes that the Superman lightning would strike twice. When this didn't happen, Siegel was quick-as-lightning fired.

Joe had an even harder time. The comic book industry was shrinking from attacks by do-gooders and competition for kids' eyeballs from television. Super heroes, so vital to the World War II period, were vanishing from the scene. Now romance, animation-inspired funny animals, Western, crime, and horror comics were competing for attention. Adding to Joe's problem was that his diagrammatic style was thought of as archaic. There were strong, second generation comic book artists like Wally Wood, Frank Frazetta, Bob Powell, and Jack Kirby filling the panels with virtuoso art.

A contemporary cartoonist of Shuster's, Gill Fox, shared with me that, "Joe became a delivery boy for a printer, and one day had to bring some printing proofs to the DC offices. The publisher, Donenfeld, spied him in the lobby, slipped him a mere twenty bucks, and instructed him to never make deliveries there again."

In early 1954, Joe's career took yet another turn. He illustrated kinky tales of adventure, bondage, and torture in sixteen booklets, *Nights of Horror,* along with a handful of other lurid titles. The publishing company was Malcla. The "Mal" of Malcla was Eugene Maletta, a printer in Queens operating out of his father's basement. In an interview for this book, Maletta recalls that the "Cla" of Malcla was a "Clancy," the writer of *Nights of Horror.* Clancy's writing for these potboilers consisted of purloining stories from old, spicy pulps. Professor of Erotology and Sexology at the Institute for Advanced Study of Human Sexuality Dr. C. J. Scheiner, who has been called "one of the world's foremost authorities on erotica," told me he met the co-publisher "Cla" (as he refers to him) when he bought his book collection. Scheiner reports that "the co-publisher detailed how he got his neighbor, the nearly blind and totally broke Shuster, to do the job and also the fate of the original drawings."

In *Nights of Horror* there was little of the heroism and virtue of Superman, but all of the villainy and tension. There was spanking, flagellation, bloodletting, humiliation, teenage sex cults, torture devices, exhibitionism, and voyeurism (not to mention lesbianism and interracial sex), though little nudity. These BDSM (bondage-discipline dominance-submission sadism-masochism) tales were an equal opportunity employer. Women were tied up, whipped, and spanked, but could eagerly be the tie-ers, whippers, and spankers, too.

The art was technically some of Joe's best. It was pure Shuster work, without assistants or ghosts. It employed fine pen-and-ink work embellished by a favorite tool of the artist's, lithographic pencil. Despite his weak eyesight handicap, Joe pushed and the results were sure

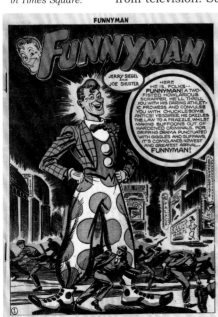

17

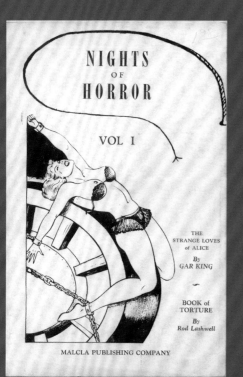

NIGHTS
OF
HORROR

VOL I

THE
STRANGE LOVES
of ALICE
By
GAR KING

BOOK of
TORTURE
By
Rod Lashwell

MALCLA PUBLISHING COMPANY

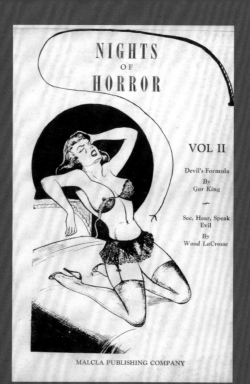

NIGHTS
OF
HORROR

VOL II

Devil's Formula
By
Gar King

See, Hear, Speak
Evil
By
Wood LaCrosse

MALCLA PUBLISHING COMPANY

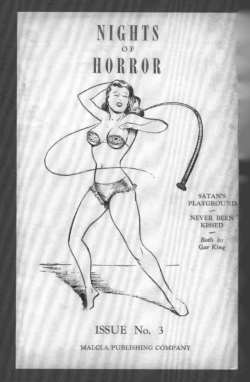

NIGHTS
OF
HORROR

SATAN'S
PLAYGROUND

NEVER BEEN
KISSED

Both by
Gar King

ISSUE No. 3

MALCLA PUBLISHING COMPANY

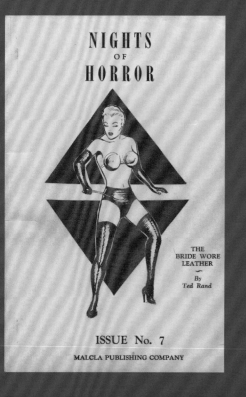

NIGHTS
OF
HORROR

THE
BRIDE WORE
LEATHER

By
Ted Rand

ISSUE No. 7

MALCLA PUBLISHING COMPANY

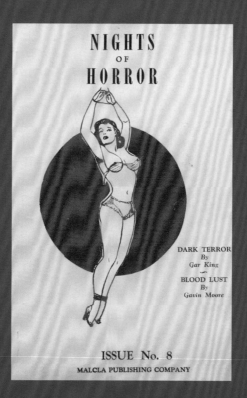

NIGHTS
OF
HORROR

DARK TERROR
By
Gar King

BLOOD LUST
By
Gavin Moore

ISSUE No. 8

MALCLA PUBLISHING COMPANY

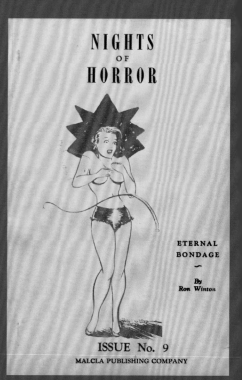

NIGHTS
OF
HORROR

ETERNAL
BONDAGE

By
Ron Winton

ISSUE No. 9

MALCLA PUBLISHING COMPANY

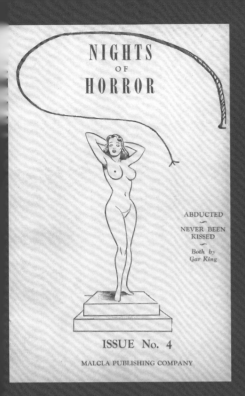

NIGHTS
OF
HORROR

ABDUCTED

NEVER BEEN
KISSED

Both by
Gar King

ISSUE No. 4

MALCLA PUBLISHING COMPANY

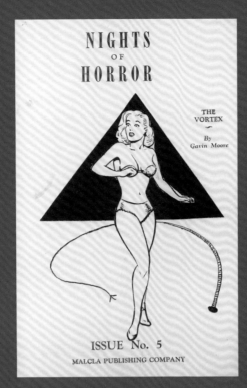

NIGHTS
OF
HORROR

THE
VORTEX

By
Gavin Moore

ISSUE No. 5

MALCLA PUBLISHING COMPANY

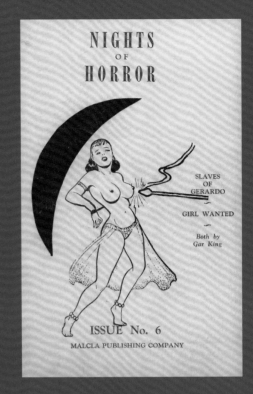

NIGHTS
OF
HORROR

SLAVES
OF
GERARDO

GIRL WANTED

Both by
Gar King

ISSUE No. 6

MALCLA PUBLISHING COMPANY

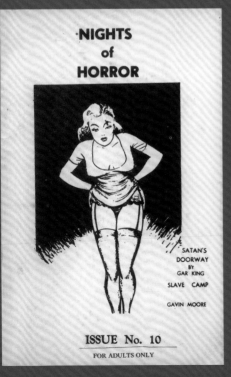

NIGHTS
of
HORROR

SATAN'S
DOORWAY
BY
GAR KING

SLAVE CAMP

GAVIN MOORE

ISSUE No. 10

FOR ADULTS ONLY

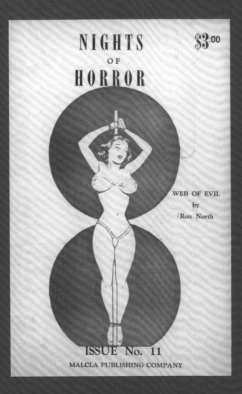

NIGHTS
OF
HORROR

$3.00

WEB OF EVIL
by
Ron North

ISSUE No. 11

MALCLA PUBLISHING COMPANY

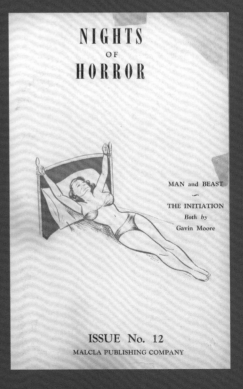

NIGHTS
OF
HORROR

MAN and BEAST

THE INITIATION
Both by
Gavin Moore

ISSUE No. 12

MALCLA PUBLISHING COMPANY

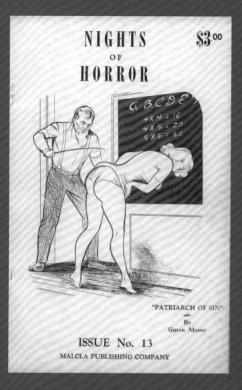

NIGHTS
OF
HORROR

$3.00

"PATRIARCH OF SIN"
By
Gavin Moore

ISSUE No. 13

MALCLA PUBLISHING COMPANY

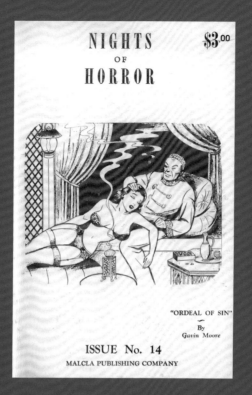

NIGHTS
OF
HORROR

$3.00

"ORDEAL OF SIN"
By
Gavin Moore

ISSUE No. 14

MALCLA PUBLISHING COMPANY

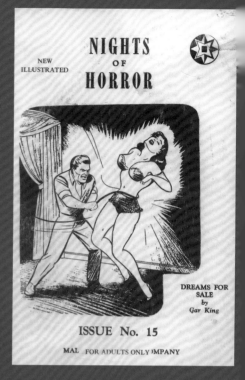

NEW
ILLUSTRATED

NIGHTS
OF
HORROR

DREAMS FOR
SALE
by
Gar King

ISSUE No. 15

MAL FOR ADULTS ONLY MPANY

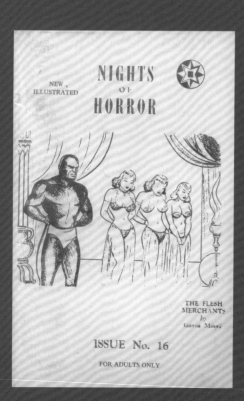

NEW
ILLUSTRATED

NIGHTS
OF
HORROR

THE FLESH
MERCHANTS
by
Gavin Moore

ISSUE No. 16

FOR ADULTS ONLY

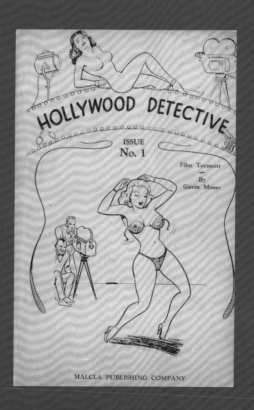

HOLLYWOOD DETECTIVE

ISSUE
No. 1

Film Torment
By
Gavin Moore

MALCLA PUBLISHING COMPANY

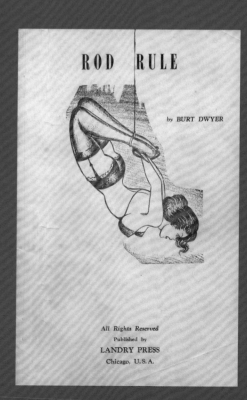

ROD RULE

by BURT DWYER

All Rights Reserved
Published by
LANDRY PRESS
Chicago, U.S.A.

and strong. Shuster always had a great ability to render attractive women, though in *Nights of Horror* they are often more sad victims than sassy vixens.

Some of the characters look like dead-ringer, bizarro versions of Superman/Clark Kent, Lois Lane, Jimmy Olsen, and Lex Luthor. Of course we know it's not really them, but these drawings smack of the citizens of Metropolis gone wild.

Marya Mannes lambasted the writing of *Nights of Horror* in *The Reporter Reader* in 1954 as "cigar store Spillane, more explicit in its sadism, more viciously saccharine in its romantic passages." The stories, like "Blood Lust," "The Flesh Merchants," and "The Bride Wore Leather," were bylined by Clancy's salacious pseudonyms, like Ted Rand, Wood LaCrosse, and Rod Lashwell. The S&M scenarios had pulp-type villains, scantily clad damsels in distress, and even a few handsome heroes, though they usually didn't get there just in the nick of time.

The 5½-by-8-inch *Nights of Horror* had the most amateur production values imaginable. The copy wasn't professionally typeset; it was right out of an ordinary typewriter with clogged-up keys. The sometimes illegible reproduction was a horror in itself. But all this actually gives *Nights of Horror* some populist appeal. The rudimentary black-and-white

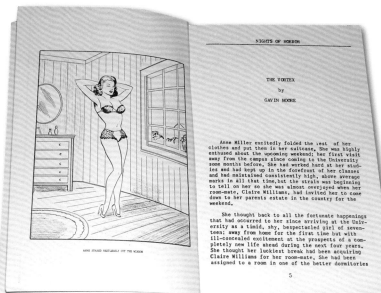

printing even foretells the feel of '60s underground comix.

When shown *Nights of Horror* illustrations, comic book historian Ron Goulart said, "I missed this phase of Joe Shuster's career the first time around. It's somewhat sad to see the guy who co-created Superman ending up drawing for what obviously must've been low-paying markets. There's no doubt that this is Shuster's work. Most of the women look like Lois Lane, though better endowed. The chap slugging the bearded lecher [pages 116–117] strikes a pose often utilized by the young Superman as well as private eye Slam Bradley in *Detective Comics*. The lad who is being led astray by the smoking blonde [page 55] looks like a jaded Jimmy Olsen."

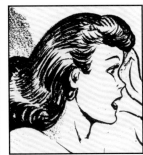

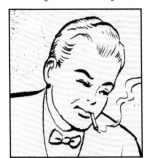

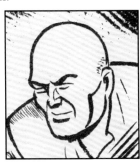

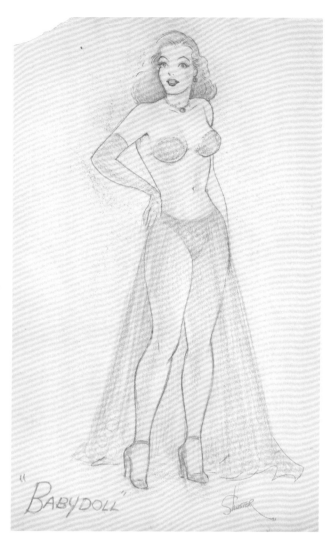

"BABYDOLL"

Bill Blackbeard, founder-director of the San Francisco Academy of Comic Art and editor of *The Smithsonian Collection of Newspaper Comics,* asserts that *Nights of Horror* is "a god-awful discovery, but obviously something done in loathing and despair to bring in desperately needed bucks. To my scalded eye, the work is undeniably Shuster's, something almost certainly undertaken for a fly-by-night publisher."

Dr. Bradley Ricca, Ph.D., from the Department of English at Case Western University and a Siegel and Shuster historian, has a more positive take. "Nowhere is Joe identified as the artist. That being said, it is definitely him. Not only in the way the squints of the eyes and jaws are drawn, but also the foreshortened limbs and the use of pencil. It is also seemingly some of his best work! This shows he wasn't completely blind at this time."

Did Joe Shuster *have* to take on *Nights of Horror*? Other comic book artists were struggling, but finding work in advertising, education, and industry. Was creating pornography an act of financial desperation? Or was drawing characters who looked like their famous counterparts, only in compromising situations, an act of retribution? Or is it possible that there was something in Joe that enjoyed this type of fantasy material?

Are there any clues to be found in what we know about Shuster's romantic relationships? We do know of a few of the women in Joe's life.

Jolan Kovacs, Joe's first muse, changed her name to Joanne Carter when she became a full-time model. She posed for painters, illustrators, and photographers in Philadelphia, Boston, and New York, and was a cigarette girl in a West Coast club. Joanne, an attractive and strong woman, was encouraging and loyal to Jerry and Joe. "To me she was Lois Lane," Joe said in an early 1980s interview. In the same article, Joanne tells of going on a date with Joe to a National Cartoonists Society costume ball. It was at the Plaza Hotel, in New York, in 1948. "Joe took me down to the Brooks costume company and rented an enormous ball gown for me so I looked exactly like Dixie Dugan [a popular comic strip character of the time known for her stylish clothes]. Jerry and Joe were having problems at the time—there was litigation—and I just didn't feel like going as Lois Lane under those circumstances." Joanne came with Joe but left with Jerry Siegel. "After this reunion at the ball, Jerry and I started dating, and a few months later, we were married."

Joanne reveals, "I never did any fashion modeling; I was never tall enough. I wanted to grow more, but this was as high as I got." Maybe her lack of height is why Joe seemed to be

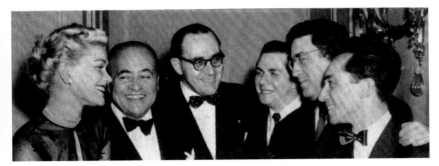

content that his "Lois" went off with Jerry rather than him after the ball.

Jerry Robinson recalls, "Joe and I double-dated a number of times. He was shy with women and I guess it's no secret to say that he loved tall, beautiful, intelligent women. I don't think that is uncommon among very short men. I think maybe it adds to their stature. I remember one time I got him a date with one of my cousins, who was a brilliant girl. I think she graduated first in her class of over one thousand students, and she was very attractive. We had a lovely evening. When we got back to my place and I said, 'Well, did you have a good time—how did you like my cousin?' Joe says, 'Oh, yeah, she was great, but she was too short.'"

Dr. Bradley Ricca interviewed Joe's sister, Jean Shuster-Peavy. She confided, "Actually, Joe loved tall, beautiful showgirls and models, and he dated a lot of them! He was what you call a 'Stagedoor Johnny.' He dated a lot of models—beautiful ones—he'd just pick the most beautiful models and girls!"

Ricca shared a little-known fact: "Joe was married in 1975 to Judy Calpini, a Las Vegas showgirl. They married in San Diego; Jerry and Joanne were there. The marriage lasted maybe only a few months, I think. That was the only time he married." This was apparently such a blip in Joe's life that, later, Joanne Carter told an interviewer, "He never married."

Whether his motive was for love or for money, Shuster could never have imagined the nights of horror that lay ahead.

Suddenly, in August 1954, *Nights of Horror* became all too real and, in fact, was blamed for

contributing to the brutal actions of a group of teenagers known as the Brooklyn Thrill Killers.

> *THRILL KILLERS VICTIM FOUND IN*
> *EAST RIVER*
> —*New York Journal American*

> *TEEN THRILL KILLERS SEIZED*
> —*Brooklyn Eagle*

> *TEEN THRILL SLAYERS BAFFLE*
> *JUDGES AND SICKEN OFFICIALS*
> —*New York World Telegram and Sun*

The slicks had slightly more time to reflect on the news that four teenagers from "good homes" flogged girls and murdered vagrants in Brooklyn parks. *Newsweek* referred to them as

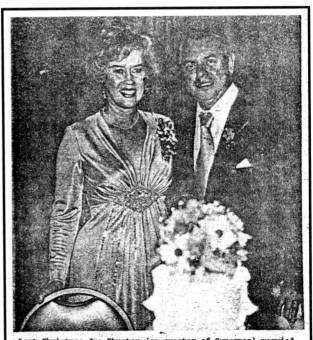

Last Christmas Joe Shuster (co-creator of Superman) married for the first time. His bride, the former Judy Calpini, is as beautiful inside as she is to look at. A former show-girl, she is a writer and artist in her own right and she and Joe are hard at work on several projects. She has done wonders for Joe, who has never looked better in his life. (Judy is into nutrition and that makes the difference.) This is truly the happy ending to the Superman story!

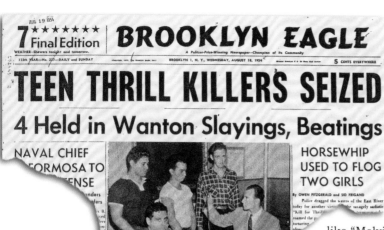

BROOKLYN EAGLE

A Pulitzer-Prize-Winning Newspaper—Champion of Its Community

WEATHER—Showers tonight and tomorrow. 115th YEAR—No. 227—DAILY and SUNDAY BROOKLYN 1, N. Y., WEDNESDAY, AUGUST 18, 1954 5 CENTS EVERYWHERE

TEEN THRILL KILLERS SEIZED

4 Held in Wanton Slayings, Beatings

NAVAL CHIEF FORMOSA TO ...ENSE

HORSEWHIP USED TO FLOG TWO GIRLS

By OWEN FITZGERALD and SID FRIGAND

Police dragged the waters of the East River today for another victim of the savagely sadistic "Kill for Thrills" termagants... roamed the p... torturing... phra...

"Those Terrible Young." "Quiet Boys and Horror," *Life* exclaimed. *Time* tried to sum it all up with a terse, one-word headline: "Senseless."

Of course the popular detective magazines of the time ate these brutal crimes up with a dirty spoon in their wordy, pulpy heads and subheads. *True Detective* read: "Thrill Kill Kids— They Roamed the Streets and Parks of Brooklyn to torture, maim, and murder for innocent fun!" And *Inside Detective* (published by Dell, the same people who gave us *Donald Duck* and *Little Lulu* comics) went back to all caps with: "BOY HITLER OF FLATBUSH AVE." Dell's subhead: "It was a torture spree of lashings, burnings, and murder that had cost two lives and maimed two others. It was fun for a gang of four mentally warped youths who killed for the thrill and respected only their leader, the eighteen-year-old who thought he was Hitler."

This was Jack Koslow, a Jewish teenager who was spouting "Heil Hitler!" when he was seven, during the Pledge of Allegiance. As the sallow redhead became tall and thin, he styled his mustache after his hero, Adolf Hitler. Koslow had a near-genius IQ and was a voracious reader of Mann, Spinoza, and Nietzsche's superman philosophy. He loathed all Americans who "won't fight and you can't lead them. Now the Germans are smart."

Koslow would snort, "I have an abstract hate for bums. I despise them. They are parasites on society and should all be removed."

Koslow's right-hand man— rather, right-fisted man—was Melvin Mittman. Mittman took a less intellectual approach, "I like to use the bums for punching bags to see how hard I can hit them." A character in comics with a name like "Melvin Mittman" would be the milquetoast type, but this hard-hitting, seventeen-year-old Jewish teen was five-foot-ten and weighed 210 pounds, all muscle. Like Shuster, he was the son of a clothing cutter. Like Koslow he wore a Hitler-style mustache. Mittman played the accordion and a number of other instruments, and was a trusted custodian of the locker room at a local Young Men's Hebrew Association.

A confused father recalled his son Jerome Lieberman, seventeen, as another talented musician. "The most fun we had was when we would play duets, him on the piano and me on the violin." His mother said Jerome "was a good boy." The neighbors echoed the words of Jerome's parents, "He never passed my store

LEFT: *Newspaper headlines screamed news of the brutal whippings and killings by the teenage Brooklyn Thrill Killers.*

BELOW: *The press loved to hate neo-Nazi teenage killer Jack Koslow with his Hitler mustache.*

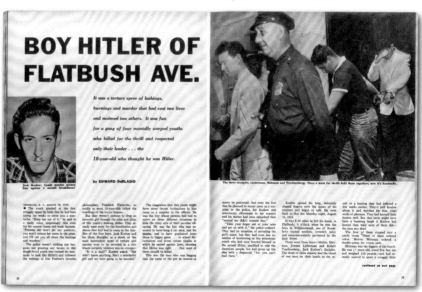

BOY HITLER OF FLATBUSH AVE.

It was a torture spree of lashings, burnings and murder that had cost two lives and maimed two others. It was fun for a gang of four mentally warped youths who killed for the thrill and respected only their leader . . . the 18-year-old who thought he was Hitler.

BY EDWARD DeBLASIO

Jack Koslow: Could murder protect him against a mental breakdown?

The three disciples, Lieberman, Mittman and Trachtenberg. Once a hunt for thrills held them together, now it's handcuffs.

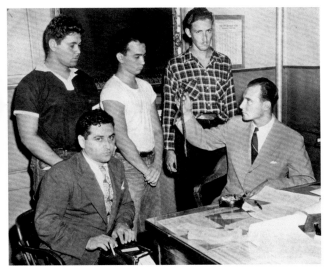

ABOVE: *Assistant D.A. Cohen holds up the bullwhip used by the Brooklyn Thrill Killers, as a stenographer takes the testimony of three of the four gang members.*

he didn't say hello." "He was always with a baseball glove—a boy plays baseball, he don't get into trouble." "He seemed like such a good boy."

The "baby" of the gang, yet the tallest, was Robert Trachtenberg, fifteen, a soft-spoken, pimply-faced boy who was referred to as "timid, quiet, polite, and unathletic." He would get uncomfortable and walk away when people got mad or raised their voices. The Trachtenberg family's flat was "clean as a whistle, you can ask the neighbors if Mrs. Trachtenberg didn't work hard bringing up that boy." When *Look* magazine queried the neighbors, they simply joined the chorus, "never no trouble, always polite, he was a good boy."

In the summer of 1954, the four teenagers terrorized Brooklyn. At night, in the parks, the gang cruelly flogged girls, mercilessly beat vagrants, and set them on fire. Reinhold Ulrickson was found with his skull cracked open and died of his injuries in the hospital, as his mother sat by. Ulrickson became the Brooklyn Thrill Killers' first murder victim. A close friend of Ulrickson's told the detectives, "I don't know who could have done this; he didn't have any enemies, and he's not the kind of man who'd go around looking for a fight."

On August 16, 1954, the boys met up at a candy store at Broadway and Marcy Avenue, in Brooklyn, not to buy super hero, crime, and horror comic books as they often did, but to plan

their evening activities. Koslow shot down the idea of going to Manhattan to look for girls, and pronounced that tonight would be another night of "bum hunting."

On their hunt, the four young thugs spied Willard Menter, an African-American, catching a few Z's on a bench in George Washington Monument Park, in the Williamsburg area of Brooklyn. Jack Koslow burned the soles of Menter's bare feet with lit cigarettes. Each time Menter cried out, Mittman smashed him in the mouth with his fist. Willard Menter was forced to walk to a pier and was pushed into the river, where he drowned. A passerby hearing the commotion quickly notified the police. A detective named Bradley, like the Siegel and Shuster character, and Bradley's partner, John Burke, caught the four teenage terrorists as they were running from the scene. Lieberman and Trachtenberg seemed relieved to confess; Mittman and Koslow, however, were boastful. Koslow proudly hailed this night of horror as his "supreme adventure."

Cartoonist Gene Basset participated at the Brooklyn Thrill Killers' trial. In my interview with him, Basset recalls, "No photography was allowed in the courtroom, so the *Brooklyn Eagle* asked me if I'd go down and do some drawings.

RIGHT: *A sad and gripping scene on the dock with the four handcuffed Brooklyn Thrill Killers pointing to their murder victim, Willard Menter, and a host of police and detectives.*

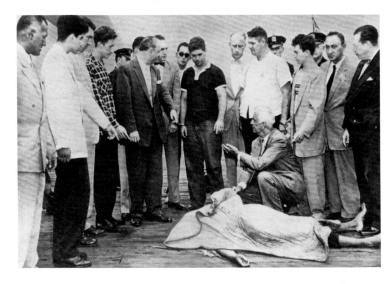

The killings were a totally aimless thrill for these teenagers. How could they turn from being Jewish to do Hitler-like things?

"They were subdued, as if going through a dream sequence, mesmerized by what was going on. It was unreal to them. Everything was somber. People were sorry to believe teenagers would pick on a vagrant, who was an easy mark, and beat him and torture him and dump him in the water.

"I was allowed to sit right next to the kids, so I could draw them. Their lawyers cleaned them up, put suits on them, and shaved their Hitler mustaches off. They were trying to put so-called best faces on them—ha! Jack Koslow was worried, quite obviously. I didn't get the idea that they were remorseful, although they were probably sorry they were there."

Trachtenberg appeared only as state's evidence. Lieberman was dismissed for lack of evidence. That left only Mittman and Koslow.

Koslow's attorney, State Senator Fred G. Moritt, who deemed his client's actions as "mischief," was a successful songwriter, and a member of ASCAP. The Senator dressed in clothes more suited for Broadway than a murder trial. He penned and recited a poem based on the children's rhyme "Ten Little Indians" for his final summation:

> Four bad boys off on
>   a spree,
> One turned State's
>   evidence, and then there
>   were three.
> Three little bad boys,
>   what did one do?
> The judge said, "No proof,"
>   and then there were two.
> Two little bad boys, in court
>   they must sit

> And pray to the Jury, "Please,
>   please acquit."

Marya Mannes reported that, after the Senator's performance, nobody in the courtroom smiled, except for Moritt and Koslow.

Jack Koslow and Melvin Mittman got life.

The press, the police, and a small army of shrinks all had their opinions as to the why's of the Brooklyn Thrill Killers' brutal actions. A leading psychiatrist in particular became a major figure in the case. To determine if Jack Koslow was insane or could stand trial, the court called in Dr. Fredric Wertham, the famed anti–comic book crusader. Wertham concluded that the teenage killer could stand trial, but the case intrigued him. Wertham asked Judge Barshaw to let him interview Koslow in the Raymond Street jail.

Koslow matter of factly told the doctor, "I am a fascist," and "I am a fascist and a white

BELOW: *A courtroom drawing of the Thrill Killers' trial by Gene Basset for the* Brooklyn Eagle *(November, 24 1954).*

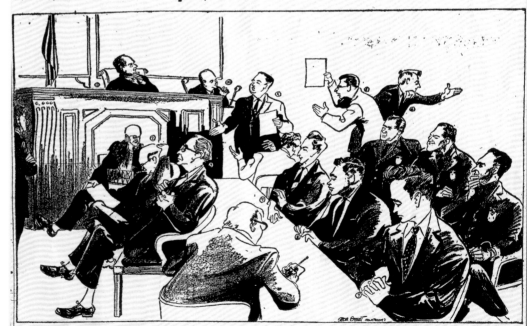

'Thrill-Killers' Open Battle to Save Lives

NIMBLE FINGERS of Brooklyn Eagle artist Gene Basset catch action in Kings County Court before Judge Hyman Barshay, as first degree murder trial of four Brooklyn teen-agers gets under way. In witness box is Joseph R. Holahan (10), first prospective juror called, who was peremptorily challenged by defense attorneys and excused. Others in sketch are (2) Defense attorney Leo Healy; (3) Defense attorney James D. C. Murray; (4) the prosecutor, Chief Assistant District Attorney J. Kenneth McCabe, questioning Holahan. Defense attorney Fred Morritt (5) and Assistant District Attorney Albert DeMeo (6) go about their tasks while the accused killers Jack Koslow (7), Melvin Mittman (8) and Jerome Lieberman (9) sit meekly at table in front of court officers.

supremacist. Violence? It's everywhere. All I'm interested in is violence, destruction, death."

Not knowing Wertham's identity, Koslow volunteered that he was an addict of horror comics. "There's some guy, a psychiatrist, who keeps saying they have a bad effect on kids. I read about it in *Reader's Digest*. Listen—I could tell that guy something!"

Wertham revealed that he was "that guy," which amused Koslow. Koslow admitted to Wertham that, like a character from the comics, he had a secret identity. The psychiatrist reported that "He went out nights dressed in a black vampire costume, carrying a bullwhip in his back pocket." Wertham learned that Koslow got both the costume and the whip through ads in *Uncanny Tales* or *Journey into Mystery*. These were Atlas comics, an imprint of the company that later became known as Marvel. Another comic book advertisement supplied the switch-blade Koslow carried.

Marya Mannes, who interviewed Dr. Fredric Wertham, commented, "The vampire suit is an old standby in horror comics, merely a more sinister version of the tight overall ritualistic uniform of the superman, good or evil." Koslow thought horror comics to be the best, and disdainfully told Wertham that his friend Mittman "likes crime comics, you know, *Superman* and all that."

The *World-Telegram & Sun* reports, "Dr. Wertham said that Koslow and his pals, as well as many other groups of hoodlums, use the rawhide whips to beat helpless girls in the parks. 'The hoodlums are beating, kicking, burning, and whipping young girls and old men. All these horrible details are to be found in most of the comic books,' the psychiatrist said. 'I wish to emphatically point out that such crimes did not exist before this comic book era.'"

Wertham brought a set of *Nights of Horror* to Koslow's cell and inquired, "Is this the sort of thing you read?" Koslow thumbed through a couple and said, "That's it." Marya Mannes

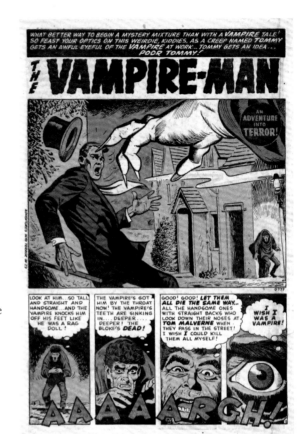

wrote, "*Nights of Horror* might leave the mature adult with no other reaction but disgust. What it might do to the immature—even the 'normal' immature—is anybody's guess. In any case it is a fact that Koslow and his companions have tried most of the refinements in the series. He even told Wertham that they made one of their beating victims kiss their feet in between blows and kicks, a scene clearly illustrated in *Nights of Horror.*" [no. 7, pages 82 and 83 of this book] "It is hardly something," said Wertham, "that a boy would do spontaneously—that is, without getting the idea from somewhere."

In the midst of all this, comic books themselves were being targeted for contributing to juvenile delinquency. In September 1954, under pressure from the government, the public, and the media, the Comic Magazine Association of America appointed as comics czar Charles Murphy to oversee the self-censorship of comic

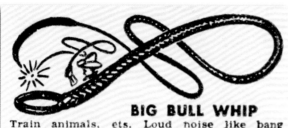

BIG BULL WHIP

Train animals, ets. Loud noise like bang of shotgun. Self defense. Do tricks Experts knock ashes off cigaret, gun out of hand, yank people off feet, etc. 4-ply hand plaited leather. Oil finished for pliability, with cracker tongue. Solid grip handle with loop.

6-ft. $1.98; 8-ft. $2.69; 10-ft. $3.29

books by publishers, eventually resulting in the Comics Code Authority.

Nights of Horror, comic books, and juvenile delinquency became entwined in the minds of the newspapers, the law, and the public. This entanglement reached its peak on February 4, 1955, when a one-day session of the New York State Joint Legislative Committee to Study the Publication of Comics was held in Manhattan. Psychiatrist Fredric Wertham was one of the main witnesses.

The Report of the NY Joint State Legislative Committee to Study the Publication of Comics 1955 proclaimed, "Few cases have stirred the nation or awakened its consciousness of juvenile delinquency as did the case of the Brooklyn 'thrill killers.' An analysis of the reading material of these boys should serve for all time as a perfect example of the contribution made to delinquency, by those who place in the hands of youth cheap, sordid, perverted, and obscene blueprints for the crimes they commit. Koslow, the leader of the gang, had read all fourteen [sic] editions of a book called *Nights of Horror,* paper-bound books selling for and portraying all types of brutality, illicit sex, and perversion."

Wertham reported his findings on Koslow to the committee. "In the course of my examination I analyzed in detail the different factors operative in this case. *Paramount as a direct, causative, contributing factor in these acts of violence was what he read.* [Italics are Wertham's for emphasis.] Koslow fancied himself as a super-man. He graduated from crime and superman comic books, which he read in his childhood. He became steeped in horror comics, his mind becoming filled with all the thrill of violence, murder, and cruelty described in them. This is not only my sober psychiatric opinion; I can prove it with objective evidence. He definitely imitated one of the stock characters of crime comic books, the 'Vampire.' He used to go out in the black costume of the vampire and roam the streets at night. On the night of the murder for which he was tried, he wore the black pants of his vampire costume."

Wertham went on to tell the committee, "In addition, he was an addict of the type of pornographic horror literature which is closely allied to comic books, although different in format. He told me he read every volume of *Nights of Horror,* and he volunteered this information at once. He said he had been fascinated and emotionally overwhelmed by them. He did not say that as an excuse; on the contrary, he mentioned it rather as something for which he felt guilty."

Wertham then showed a chart comparing "in detail the text and pictures of *Nights of Horror* with the activities of the 'thrill-killers,' and with the actual expressions [like "supreme adventure"] they used. The parallelism is complete." Wertham concluded, "In my opinion, if the community does not completely abolish the sale of crime and horror comic books and all the type of literature of *Nights of Horror* to children, all attempts to curb this kind of violent crime by young people are sheer hypocrisy of self deception. It is deeply shocking to me as a psychiatrist and criminologist that two boys have to spend the rest of their lives in jail while the profiteers of this instigating material are not even fined two dollars. They are not only accessories but, in a strictly scientific sense, they incite the youngsters to these acts."

In the days after the Brooklyn Thrill Killers' arrest, the New York police went into action. They set up a dragnet that netted hundreds of "punks," as the newspapers called them, in the

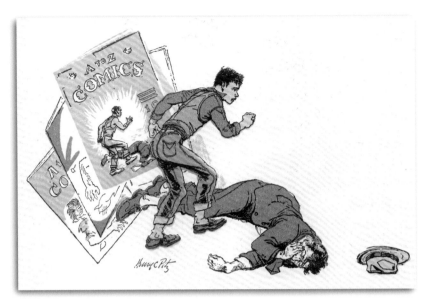

hope that this would show that New York was not helpless in the face of a deadly juvenile delinquent crime spree.

In addition, New York attacked on the legal front. On September 8, 1954, Mayor Robert Wagner announced a campaign to clean up the bookstores of "objectionable books, comics, magazines, and other publications that teach lust, violence, perverted sex attitudes, and disregard for law and order." Wagner's legal arm, the Corporation Counsel of New York, wanted a test case to see how well newly passed obscenity laws would fare in cleaning up the city. They needed a book that had all the elements Wagner spoke of, one they knew had a direct correlation to both juvenile and heinous crimes.

Nights of Horror perfectly fit the bill.

The Corporation Counsel of the City of New York filed a court motion two days after Wagner's decree and, on September 10, 1954, asked for an injunction resulting in an outright ban of the sale of *Nights of Horror*. Corporation Counsel Adrian P. Burke wrote in the motion, "A survey has been made by the Police department and the Law department of the City of the obscene, lewd, lascivious, filthy, indecent, and disgusting 'literature' accessible to the youth of our City. The *Nights of Horror* publication is a flagrant example of such 'literature.' Adhering to the old

adage that 'a picture is worth a thousand words,' the author leaves nothing for the unimaginative mind to visualize by itself. The many 'illustrations' that embellish these stories serve to arouse the few abnormal sexual emotions that might have remained dormant during the reading of the tortures, the flagellation, the sadism, the masochism. All are graphically pictured in such a way as to cause unnatural desire, culminating, often times, in unnatural and vicious acts. Violence, unrestrained and unnatural, is their keynote."

The police commissioner of the City of New York, F. W. H. Adams, corroborated, "It is the informed opinion of those police officials, whose professional lives have been dedicated to the fight against crime, that there is a definite relationship between the types of crime portrayed in *Nights of Horror* and similar works, and the crimes of sex and violence which beset the City of New York today. It is their informed opinion that at least one of the causes of today's crimes of sex and violence is the dissemination among the youth today of literature of the genre of *Nights of Horror*. If the ultimate relief sought by the Corporation Counsel is granted, it will be possible to prevent publication and distribution of *Nights of Horror*. This will be a significant step to our continuing fight against crime in New York City."

The Deputy Police Commissioner in Charge of the Juvenile Aid Bureau, James B. Nolan, added, "*Nights of Horror* treats sexual perversion as a normal way of life."

Captain Henry J. Mulhearn further stated, "The viciousness of these publications transgresses the bounds of decency."

On September 13, 1954, the *New York Telegram and Sun* added kerosene to the soon-to-be-lit bonfire. It reported Assistant Corporate Counsel Milton Mollen stating, "Some kids have mouthed phrases and words from *A Night of Horror* [sic] when picked up by police for kicking, beating, and torturing younger children." Mollen said that they had evidence of

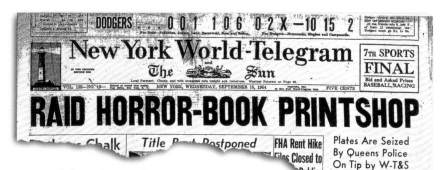

Nights of Horror's impact on juvenile crime as far back as June 1954, when the books apparently first became available.

Though these statements were presented as concern for the youth, the Corporation Counsel of New York was not content to attempt to limit the sales of *Nights of Horror* to adults only. Full censorship, outright banning of *Nights of Horror,* was the goal. Captain Henry J. Mulhearn wrote, "The granting of an injunction order is the only sure and adequate method of permanently eradicating these vile publications and keeping them from demoralizing our youth."

A front-page article by Judith Crist in the *New York Herald Tribune* reported that Corporation Counsel Burke successfully obtained a court order, the first of its kind. Supreme Court Justice Edgar J. Nathan, Jr., prevented five Times Square book shops—Kingsley Books, Metropolitan Book Shop, Times Square Book Shop, Pelley Book Shop, and Publisher's Outlet—from distributing or selling *Nights of Horror.*

No less than eighty detectives were put on the case, and the police raided Kingsley Books at 220 West 42nd Street in Times Square. These Dick Tracys found 2,650 copies of *Nights of Horror* under sheets of brown wrapping paper in the basement, and seized them all.

Kingsley Books and the Times Square Book Shop appealed to the New York State Court on Halloween 1955. After "a reading of several issues of *Nights of Horror,* the studies and reports of the New York State Joint Legislative Committee to Study the Publication of Comics, of the Special United States Senate Judiciary Sub-Committee on Juvenile Delin-

quency, and everyday observations of the shocking rise of juvenile delinquency," Judge Matthew M. Levy ruled that "public interests plead for the suppression of these publications," and that they represent "a clear and present danger."

The judge stated that in *Nights of Horror* "there is no dissemination of lawful ideas—rather there is a direct incitement to sex crime and the sordid excitement of brutality. These booklets are sold indiscriminately to all who may wish to purchase them—men and women, adults, and youths of both sexes. The publications have a libidinous effect upon ordinary, normal, healthy persons; their effect on the abnormal individual may be disastrous to him and to others as well. Incidental training of the teenager to narcotic addiction and sexual perversion was part of the activities engaged in.

"These booklets are not sex literature, as such, but pornography, unadulterated by plot, moral, or writing style. That there is no attempt to achieve any literary standard is obvious. Each issue has a suggestive sex drawing on the front cover under the caption *Nights of Horror.*"

The judge also took off for spelling: "The volumes are replete with misspelled words, typographical errors, faulty grammar, misplaced pages, and generally poor workmanship. Were the *Nights of Horror* works which indicated the slightest effort to contribute to our culture or knowledge, I might find myself in the position of 'holding my nose with one hand' and 'upholding with the other the right of free speech.'"

The judge didn't appreciate Shuster's art:

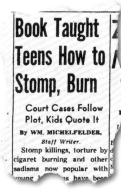

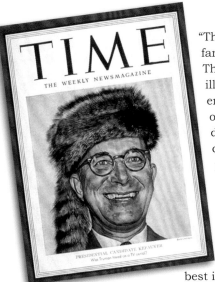

ABOVE: *Senator Kefauver's career was capped off when he was a* Time *magazine cover boy (March 24, 1952).*

"The authors have left nothing to fantasy or the unimaginative mind. The volumes are vividly detailed and illustrated. The many drawings that embellish these stories are obviously intended to arouse unnatural desire and vicious acts. Violence—criminal, sexual—degradation and perversion are the sole keynote.

"I would not want or (if I could avoid it) permit this court to become a censor, a book-burner. But a judicial tribunal should not and cannot avoid its responsibility. It was not considered in the best interest of the State to have jail cells overcrowded, be it with publishers and distributors who have violated Penal Law or with teenagers and others whose latent, abnormal emotions have become aroused by such lascivious and vicious material as that makes up the *Nights of Horror.* The legislative intent and purpose are to keep such books as the *Nights of Horror* from the impressionable public. While this court has sufficient confidence in the people of this state to feel that *Nights of Horror* can never survive, the immediate and long-range public interests were thought by the Legislature to require that the death blow be hastened."

Not content to lay down and play dead, Kingsley Books took the case all the way to the Supreme Court on April 22, 1957.

The Supreme Court verdict was handed down on June 24. There was a close decision of five to four. Delivering the opinion of the Court, Justice Felix Frankfurter, a founder of the American Civil Liberties Union, declared the booklets to be "clearly obscene, dirt for dirt's sake." The Supreme Court ruled against the distribution of *Nights of Horror,* and ordered their immediate destruction.

In a dissenting opinion, Justice Hugo Black said, "This is not a criminal obscenity case. Nor is it a case ordering the destruction of materials disseminated by a person who has been convicted of an offense for doing so, as would be authorized under provisions in the laws of New York and other States. It is a case wherein the New York police, under a different state statute, located books which, in their opinion, were unfit for public use because of obscenity, and then obtained a court order for their condemnation and destruction. The majority opinion sanctions this proceeding. I would not. Unlike the criminal cases decided today, this New York law places the book on trial."

Black continued, "There is totally lacking any standard in the statute for judging the book in context. The personal element basic to the criminal laws is entirely absent. In my judgment, the same object may have wholly different impact depending upon the setting in which it is placed. Under this statute, the setting is irrelevant. It is the manner of use that should determine obscenity. It is the conduct of the individual that should be judged, not the quality of art or literature. To do otherwise is to impose a prior restraint, and hence to violate the Constitution. Certainly, in the absence of a prior judicial determination of illegal use, books, pictures, and other objects of expression should not be destroyed." Justice Hugo Black concluded, "It savors too much of book burning."

In another dissenting opinion, Justice William Douglas called the banning of *Nights of Horror* "censorship at its worst."

Judith Crist, who went on to become a famed film critic, interviewed Dr. Fredric Wertham about comic books for *Colliers* and wrote about *Nights of Horror* for the *New York Herald Tribune* in the '50s. Crist now reflects in an interview for *Secret Identity,* "The censorship that zealots like Dr. Fredric Wertham encouraged was part of the times, as the immediate post–World War II euphoria faded. By the mid-'50s in addition to the 'pornography' hearings of Senator Estes Kefauver with Wertham, re-fueled by his 1954 book, *Seduction of the Innocent,* as a star witness, we had 'black listing' of artists and the Communist witch hunts of Senator Joseph McCarthy. Censorship was deplorable paranoia and blame-casting."

Critics of comic books, Superman, and the Brooklyn Thrill Killers' supreme adventure reprehensibly didn't seem concerned with the Supreme Court's book banning decision, where "the democratic ideals that we should seek are likely to be overlooked."

A *New York World-Telegram* article citing Koslow's reading of *Nights of Horror* was pivotal in the police investigation of the publishing of these booklets. A woman reader contacted the *World-Telegram* to rat out the man who was the printer, her relative Eugene Maletta. In the early '50s, Maletta opened a small, struggling print shop, Pilgrim Press, in Queens. On September 15, 1954, detectives swooped into Pilgrim Press and arrested Maletta while he was printing *Nights of Horror*.

In a 2008 interview for this book, Maletta said he became the printer of *Nights of Horror* when Clancy "came to me and asked me if we split fifty-fifty, if I'd do it, so I did." Eugene declares, "There was a ready market for it, that was for sure, that's why we came out with sixteen titles." Maletta contends that the print run of each book was "just one thousand, maybe we reprinted one or two, but I don't remember when." Asked if he had ever met the artist, Joe Shuster, Maletta claims, "I had nothing to do with that—I just printed them," though he did add, "I think we paid about $100 for the artwork per book."

After the Brooklyn Thrill Killers' crimes, Mayor Wagner's campaign against smut, and the damning testimony to the New York State Joint Legislative Committee, *Nights of Horror* was not yet finished in the public eye. The United States Senate was now circling above the notorious booklets.

Senator Estes Kefauver (D) of Tennessee, a presidential hopeful, was famous for campaigning in a coonskin cap. There was not a lurid

topic which he did not want to hold hearings about. He was already famous for his Senate subcommittee hearings on crime, comic books, and juvenile delinquency. In the spring of 1955, Kefauver decided to add pornography to his portfolio, and take the act on the road. First stop: New York City.

In preparation for these hearings, "Pornography and its Effects on Juvenile Delinquency," Senator Kefauver enlisted the aid of Police Lieutenant George Butler from Dallas, Texas, to investigate the correlation between juveniles and pornography. Lieutenant Butler set up a meeting on April 28, 1955, with New York City officials, including District Attorney Frank S. Hogan and Corporation Counsel member Milton Mollen.

Mollen divulged that they did not get the racketeer behind *Nights of Horror*. Mollen's investigation fingered a Jewish pornographer with alleged ties to the Gambino family, co-owner of Kingsley Books and a handful of other Times Square bookshops: Edward Mishkin. The hearing revealed, "Sources indicated that Eddie Mishkin is 'Mr. Big' in the midtown pornography racket."

Edward, Ed, Eddie Mishkin, a "Sultan of Smut," as reporter Thomas Collins, Jr., called him, came into the world in 1909, and was arrested before he was thirty for bookmaking. Mishkin eventually achieved a level of infamy for being the promoter of a film that became known as "The Pork Lady," about the romantic relations between a Swedish lady and her pig. In 1960, District Attorney Frank S. Hogan anointed Mishkin "the

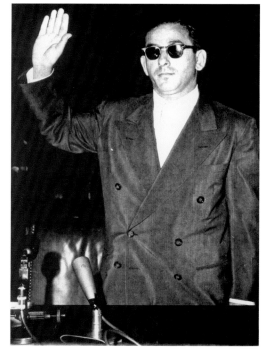

BELOW: *Jewish mobster and "Sultan of Smut" Eddie Mishkin swearing in at Senator Kefauver's hearings on "Pornography and its Effects on Juvenile Delinquency" (1955).*

Accused of Filth, Four Use the Fifth

By SIDNEY KLINE

A dramatic expose of sordid interstate traffic in pornography was climaxed in the Federal Building, Foley Square, yesterday by the summoning to the witness stand of several men described as key distributors or dealers in filthy movies, pictures and writings.

Four of the "business men"—all of them on hand under subpena—clammed up on their operations under the Constitutional right to refuse to testify against themselves. But law enforcement officers spoke freely about the business.

250G Ring Crushed

...istant U. S. Attorney ...r of Baltimore, de...ing of a $250,000-...a-year r..... the FBI. Three men were convicted. They were Herman Solomon, Raymond Daymont and Louis Passetti. Solomon, said Bair, used an apartment at 224 W. 49th St. as a studio in which to photograph models.

...he four who hid behind the ...Amendment were Abraham...

Edward Mishkin at yesterday's hearing.

(NEWS foto by Arthur Buck...)

...graphic pict... stance b...

"Pornography is more dangerous than narcotics," said Blick earnestly. He urged that the cops be given the same search and seizure powers in their fight on pornography as narcotics law provide in the battle again dope.

Blick told of a raid he March 28, 1953, on a Washin... dance studio, where he found boys 11 years old and up wa... to see an obscene movie. The was traced to Fodor.

"Erroneous Impression"

During the day's procee... James H. Bobo, general c... to the subcommittee, ann... that he wanted to clear "erroneous impression" of some accounts of ... hearing on -Tuesd... 220-59 73d A... ghost ...... Pat co... k... a... f...

largest producer and purveyor of pornographic material in the U.S., and at that time he was pulling in 1.5 million dollars a year."

How bad was Mishkin? Lex Luthor bad. In a behind-the-scenes, May 24, 1955, confidential memo uncovered for this book, Lieutenant Butler paints him as an evil scumbag: "Mishkin is very secretive. A man named 'Hymie' had intended to put Mishkin on the spot and take over the racket. Eddie hired two thugs to run over Hymie with a car and kill him. Mishkin's flagellation series of sex perversion, the *Nights of Horror,* contains every known type of sexual perversion. Mishkin is regarded as the 'Papa' in this field. He is allegedly a pervert himself."

The memo continues, "Much of Mishkin's success can be traced, according to the informer, to 'arrangements' he has with law enforcement sources. His 'ice' is distributed by Mishkin on two levels, the precinct and the division. $1,000 a month is reportedly paid to the Division Chief. $500 a month to the Precinct Chief. Then there are twenty men on their squads who get $20 per month each. The informer has not actually seen a payoff but he has been in the stores when the police call for their money. He said they were taken to the back of the store, behind a partition, and paid off. On the days when the payments were made it looked like a police parade."

Kefauver's stage was the United States Courthouse in New York City, where he held his hearings from May 26 to June 1, 1955. Both Eugene Maletta and Edward Mishkin were called to testify. Mishkin was grilled about his involvement in pornography and *Nights of Horror.* Maletta was grilled about how he went from being broke to being worth over $40,000, owning his home, two cars, and valuable printing equipment in just three years.

Both Mishkin and Maletta refused to cooperate, pleading the Fifth to all pertinent questions. A Contempt of Congress citation was drawn up against Mishkin, but not voted on by the Senate.

Mishkin found himself in court repeatedly. In a 1965 trial, an author contracted by Mishkin testified that, "The sex had to be very strong, it had to be rough, it had to be clearly spelled out. Sex scenes had to be unusual sex scenes between men and women, and women and women, and men and men. He wanted scenes in which women were making love with women. There were spankings and scenes, sex in an abnormal and irregular fashion." Another writer testified that Mishkin instructed him "to deal very graphically with the darkening of the flesh under flagellation."

A court summary reported that, "Artists in the trial testified in similar vein as to appellant's instructions regarding illustrations and covers for the books."

The judge stated that Mishkin's publications "get into the hands of small, limited minds, and they [get] worked up to a fever pitch, and some poor soul is the victim." In 1954, the government worried that the small, limited minds included marauding juvenile delinquents preying on poor souls they found in Brooklyn parks. In the 1965 trial, the judge sentenced Mishkin to three years at Rikers Island, where he was incarcerated on weekends. He continued his smut activities during the week. According to the Department of Justice in their 1977 report, "Organized Crime Involvement in Pornography," Mishkin went on to become "one of the nation's largest producers, manufacturers, and distributors of pornography."

During the mid-'50s crackdown on *Nights of Horror,* Clancy, co-publisher/writer, was feeling the pressure. Pornography historian J. B. Rund relates that "Clancy packed up the original art and manuscripts in a suitcase and threw them into the Long Island Sound."

A few surviving stories, which may have been slated for future editions of *Nights of Horror,* were soon published under different titles, like *Hollywood Detective* and *Rod Rule.*

Some forbidden copies of *Nights of Horror* survived. The covers were torn off and different covers were affixed, bearing the titles *Pink Chemise* and *Black Chemise.* Unbeknownst to the authorities, these "new" books were then

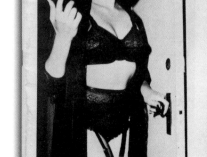

sold under the disguise of their "secret identity."

There was another risqué and pornographic periodical with illustrations by Shuster, the undated *Continental* magazine, a slick digest. Between the pages of bondage photos, Shuster illustrated articles and created a four-page comic book story

starring Annette, Secret Agent Z-4. Joe ended this strip with the phrase, "continued in next issue." It never was.

Later, Shuster drew up a few saucy greeting card ideas, but they were never published. The artist did, however, sell a few mild gag cartoons to girlie humor digests, like *Jest,* in the early '60s. In a interview for this book, cartoonist Bob Weber recounted that editor Albert Sulman told him, "Look at these cartoons signed 'Josh.' Who do you think these are by?" When Bob said he didn't know, the editor proudly proclaimed, "Joe Shuster!" The "Jo" in "Josh" was from Joe, the "sh" from Shuster. Joe was josh-ing.

Just before the first Superman movie, an impoverished Jerry Siegel wrote a press release/screed, putting a curse on the movie. Fans, cartoonists (led by Jerry Robinson), and the media pressured DC Comics, which eventually began to pay Siegel and Shuster a modest salary, health benefits, and returned their credits to the comic books.

In 1992, Shuster died at age seventy-eight in Los Angeles.

The book burning of *Nights of Horror* by the Supreme Court, along with its low print run and distribution possibly only in Times Square for a few months, make this material extremely rare. Few people have ever seen it. Certainly the fistful of shrinks, journalists, police, and politicos who did, thankfully, never made the connection between *Nights of Horror* and the co-creator of Superman.

The ties between *Nights of Horror,* the Brooklyn Thrill Killers, the arrest of Eugene Maletta, the pursuit of Edward Mishkin, the Kingsley Books trial, and the Senate investigations must have created some nights of horror

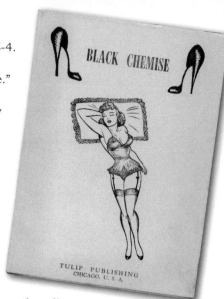

ABOVE: Nights of Horror *issue no. 16's alter ego,* Black Chemise. *The "Tulip Publishing, Chicago, U.S.A." is probably a ruse.*

LEFT: *In the digest* Continental, *Shuster illustrated articles like, "Man Is Master, "A Woman's World," "Panty Raids," "Old Fashioned," and "Judge's Ruling."*

for Joe Shuster. But until now, there hasn't been any revelation of Shuster's involvement in these events. Shuster must have been relieved when the critics, the public, the police, the feds, the national magazines, and the New York newspapers eventually turned their attention to other matters.

Superman is the first and greatest costumed super hero. But it is well known that, as a fictional character, he has one flaw: He's perfect. This often makes Superman hard to write for and sometimes hard to relate to. Today, at least, we like our heroes with some imperfections—we can better empathize.

Joe Shuster's lifelong close friend Jerry Siegel (who died on January 28, 1996) can give us a good summation of the essence of the artist's work and the artist himself. Siegel wrote that Shuster's Superman "was absolutely inspired. There was a nobility, a grace, a force of sheer power, an imaginativeness, a touch of class, a drama, a glint of humor, that reflected certain unique elements in the character of Joe himself."

Joe Shuster was all that and more. The revelation that Joe had a secret identity who created porn will upset some people. But this imperfection, if his alter ego is that, makes him far more a person of interest—someone we, with our own flaws, can relate to. There might even be something in these pen-and-ink perversions that we can find intriguing, if not engaging.

Shuster was a poor immigrant with rich ideas. Those rich ideas took him to wealth, then back to poverty. It's a rags-to-riches-to-rags story. Joe became a warning for creators to not undersell their ideas, and the poster child for starving artists. Whether *Nights of Horror* started as a paycheck or a passion, they resulted in super manic weeks and months of horror, when fiction became terrifying fact on the streets of Brooklyn.

Up, up, and awry.

Superman was introduced as the Man of Tomorrow. But tomorrow is today. Some things have changed; some remain the same. Reviled comic books have become respected graphic novels. Brooklyn=Columbine. Wertham's "direct, causative, contributing factor in these acts of violence" is now video games. Bondage-inspired fashion is de rigueur on Catwoman and on the catwalk. Our First Amendment freedoms still are sometimes scarily tenuous. Yet porn isn't under the counter in a sleazy bookstore in Times Square, but is potentially on the laps of everyone with an Internet connection. Times Square itself has gone from sadism to the Happiest Place on Earth. Truth, justice, and the American way are now truthiness, O.J., and "We've lost our way."

When I found a *Nights of Horror* booklet in a dusty old cardboard box in a used bookseller's stall, these words leaped in a single bound to my mind: "Oh, my God, Joe Shuster!" At a lunch meeting I had with a super-high comic book exec, I took out this same *Nights of Horror* and handed it across the table to him. Faster than anything he gasped, "Oh, my God, Joe Shuster!"

Now that some of the few remaining books that were saved from the censor's fire have been exhumed, you too can join the chorus and say, "Oh, my God . . ."

BELOW: *In the early 1960s, Joe Shuster drew girlie cartoons for low-rent digests published by Humorama. Shuster used the pseudonym "Josh" (the "Jo" is from Joe and the "sh" from Shuster). In this cartoon Joe chose to create a gag about spanking. While there's a humorous side to this cartoon, the art technique and subject matter match the illustrations of* Nights of Horror.

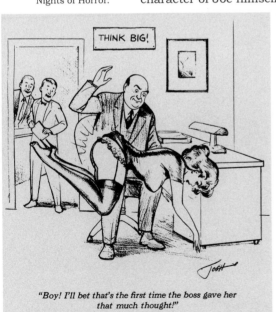

THINK BIG!

"Boy! I'll bet that's the first time the boss gave her that much thought!"

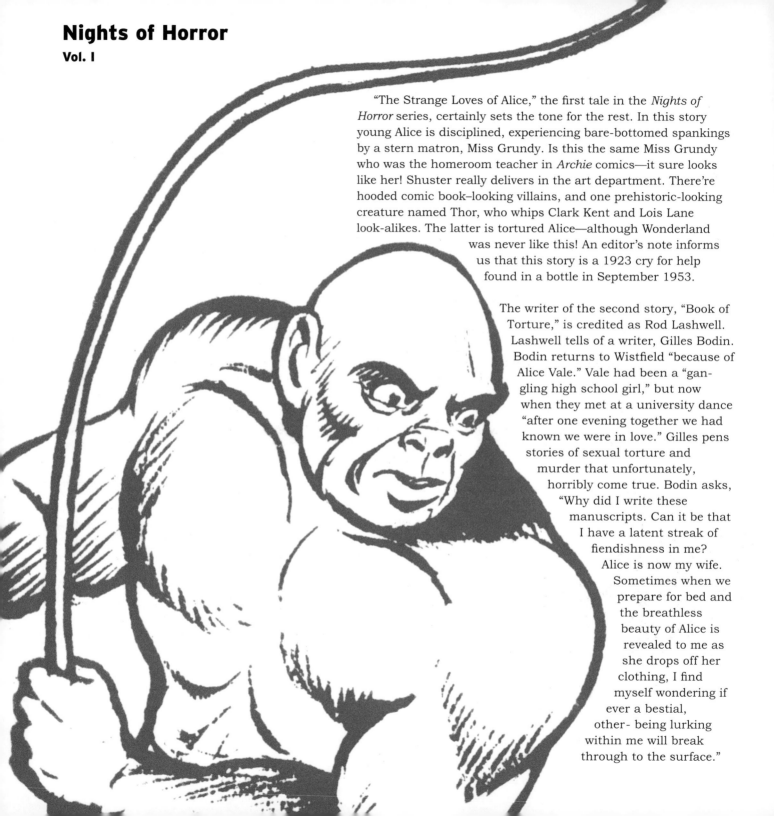

Nights of Horror
Vol. I

"The Strange Loves of Alice," the first tale in the *Nights of Horror* series, certainly sets the tone for the rest. In this story young Alice is disciplined, experiencing bare-bottomed spankings by a stern matron, Miss Grundy. Is this the same Miss Grundy who was the homeroom teacher in *Archie* comics—it sure looks like her! Shuster really delivers in the art department. There're hooded comic book–looking villains, and one prehistoric-looking creature named Thor, who whips Clark Kent and Lois Lane look-alikes. The latter is tortured Alice—although Wonderland was never like this! An editor's note informs us that this story is a 1923 cry for help found in a bottle in September 1953.

The writer of the second story, "Book of Torture," is credited as Rod Lashwell. Lashwell tells of a writer, Gilles Bodin. Bodin returns to Wistfield "because of Alice Vale." Vale had been a "gangling high school girl," but now when they met at a university dance "after one evening together we had known we were in love." Gilles pens stories of sexual torture and murder that unfortunately, horribly come true. Bodin asks, "Why did I write these manuscripts. Can it be that I have a latent streak of fiendishness in me? Alice is now my wife. Sometimes when we prepare for bed and the breathless beauty of Alice is revealed to me as she drops off her clothing, I find myself wondering if ever a bestial, other- being lurking within me will break through to the surface."

"The Strange Loves of Alice"

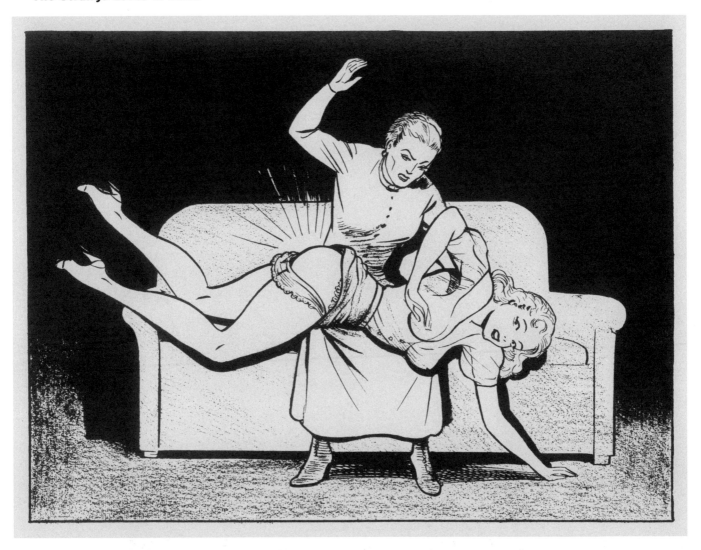

"I seemed to crave this treatment no matter how harsh or humiliating."

(Speaking of striking, many of the blondes Shuster pictured throughout the Nights of Horror *series bear a striking resemblance to Lucy Lane, Lois's sister.)*

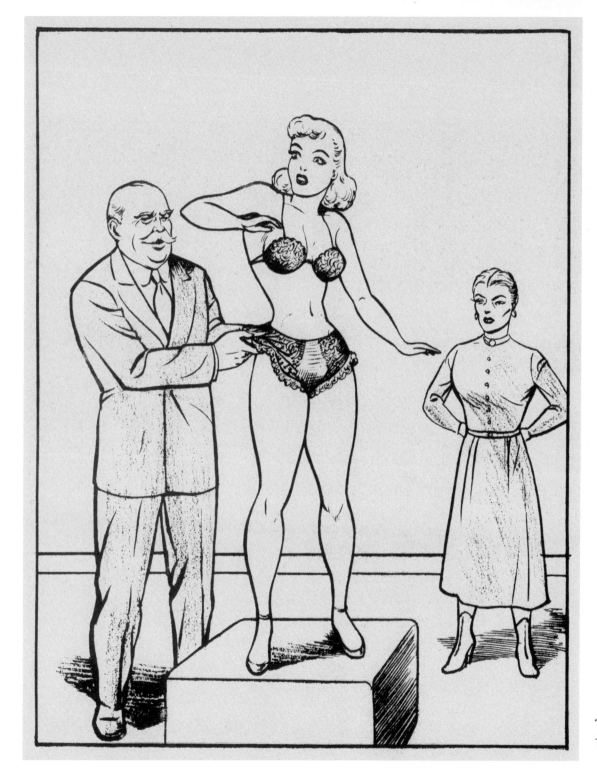

"I shuddered as I felt his fingers touch my flesh."

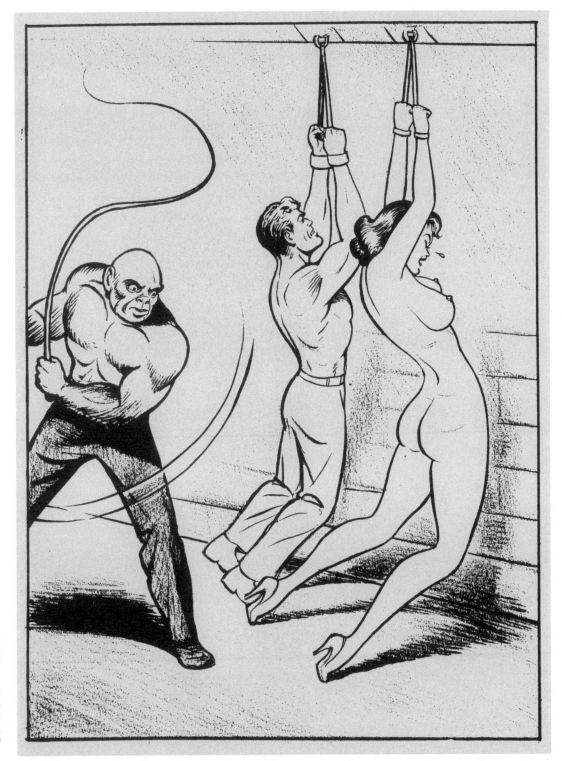

Retrieving the whip he had dropped, he began to whip and lash the both of us.

(The victims of this comic book–style villain look not unlike Superman and Lois Lane.)

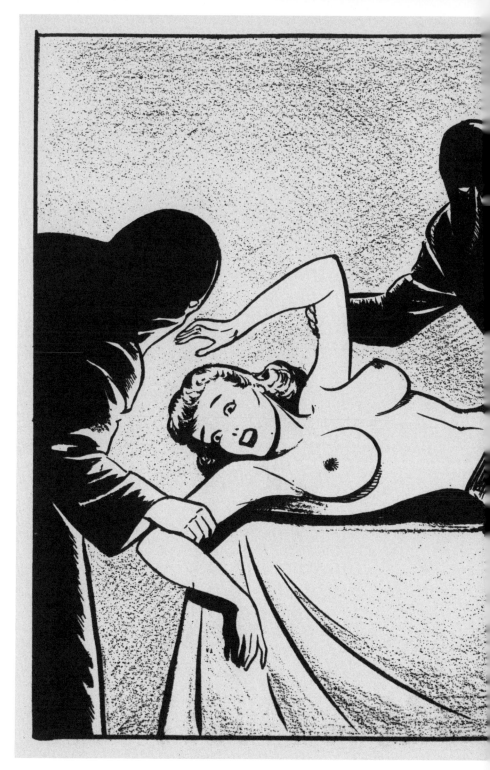

They raised my arm and stuck me with something sharp, a hypodermic, I think, for shortly after, I experienced the most wonderful feeling.

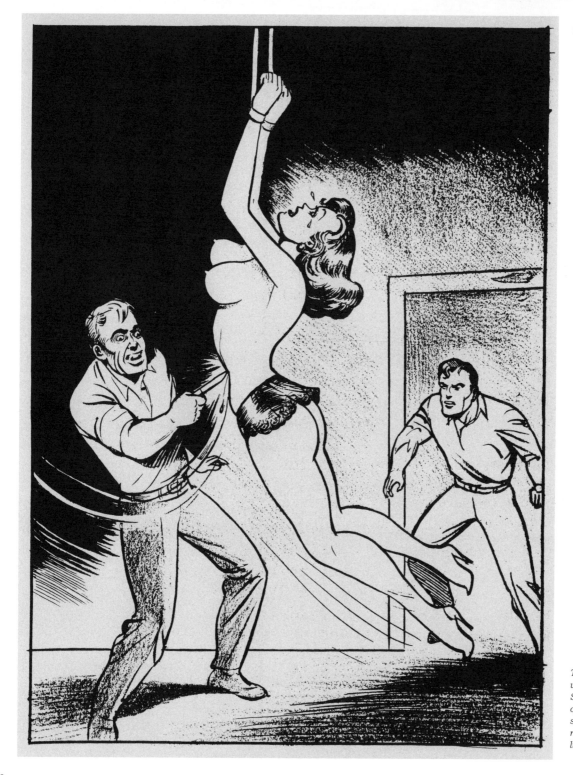

The blade went under her skin. Soon, in a matter of seconds, the skin would be ripped from her living flesh.

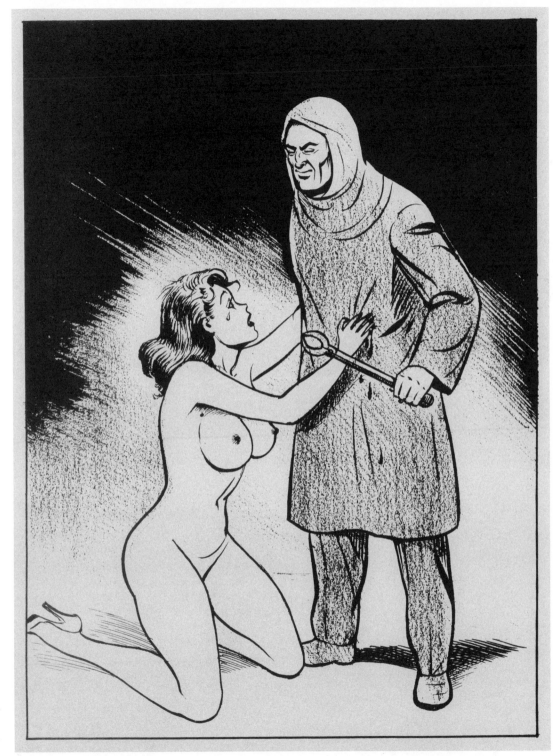

She promised all sorts of pleasure and delight to me if I would but spare her further torment.

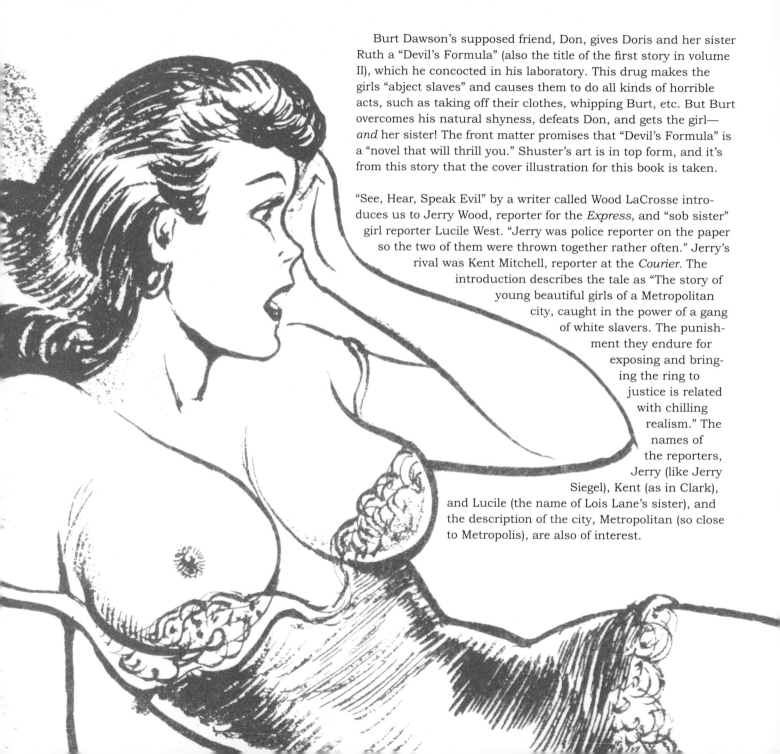

Nights of Horror
Vol. II

Burt Dawson's supposed friend, Don, gives Doris and her sister Ruth a "Devil's Formula" (also the title of the first story in volume II), which he concocted in his laboratory. This drug makes the girls "abject slaves" and causes them to do all kinds of horrible acts, such as taking off their clothes, whipping Burt, etc. But Burt overcomes his natural shyness, defeats Don, and gets the girl— *and* her sister! The front matter promises that "Devil's Formula" is a "novel that will thrill you." Shuster's art is in top form, and it's from this story that the cover illustration for this book is taken.

"See, Hear, Speak Evil" by a writer called Wood LaCrosse introduces us to Jerry Wood, reporter for the *Express,* and "sob sister" girl reporter Lucile West. "Jerry was police reporter on the paper so the two of them were thrown together rather often." Jerry's rival was Kent Mitchell, reporter at the *Courier.* The introduction describes the tale as "The story of young beautiful girls of a Metropolitan city, caught in the power of a gang of white slavers. The punishment they endure for exposing and bringing the ring to justice is related with chilling realism." The names of the reporters, Jerry (like Jerry Siegel), Kent (as in Clark), and Lucile (the name of Lois Lane's sister), and the description of the city, Metropolitan (so close to Metropolis), are also of interest.

"Devil's Formula"

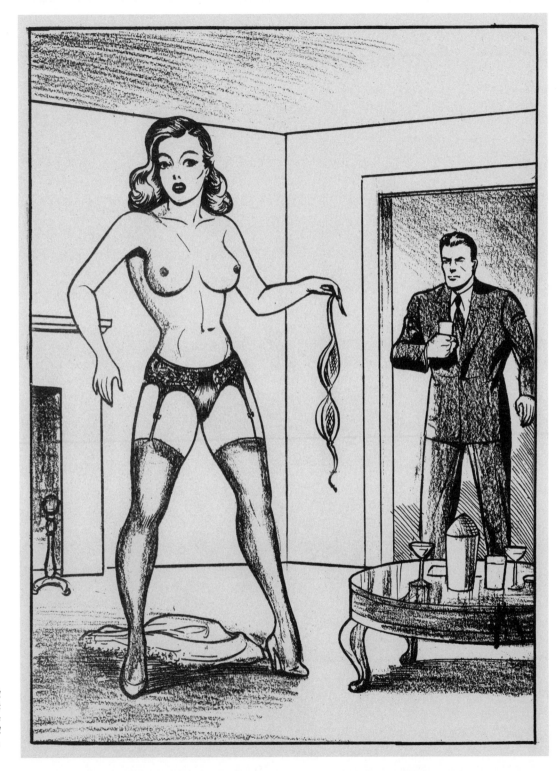

Shock and gathering lust was on Burt's face—he started towards her . . .

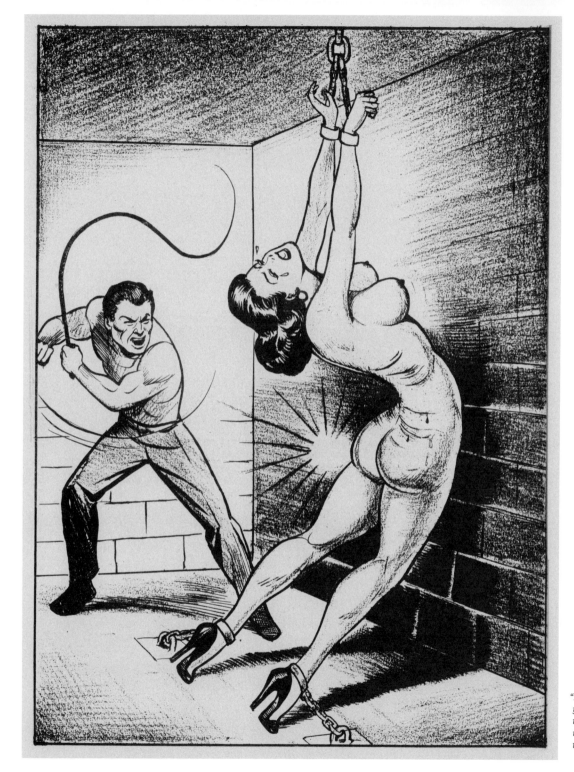

"My little slave, you should learn to obey if you wish to escape these caresses."

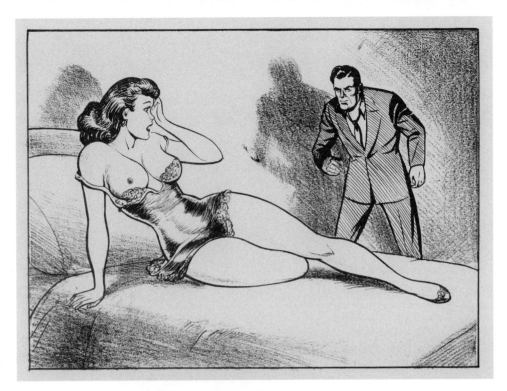

"What—what are you doing here?"

"See, Hear, Speak Evil"

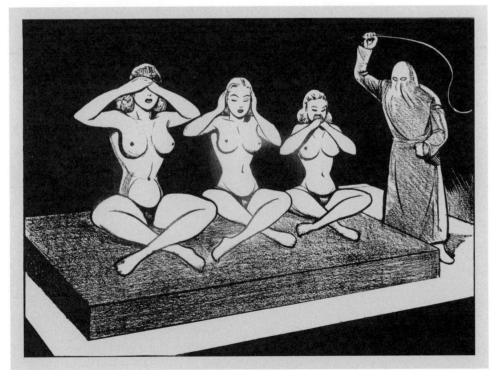

Mitchell cried, "The three wise monkeys of China—see no evil, hear no evil, speak no evil. Only . . ." "Only they're not monkeys," Jerry supplied.

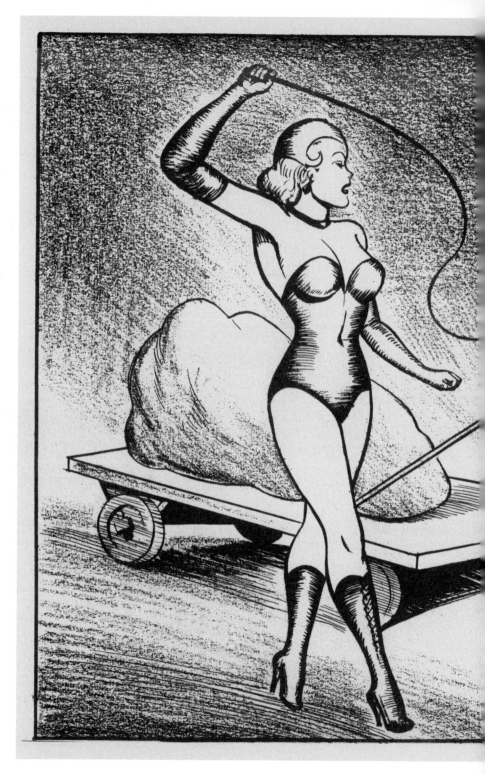

*Jerry had seen exotic dances
before, but never one like this.*

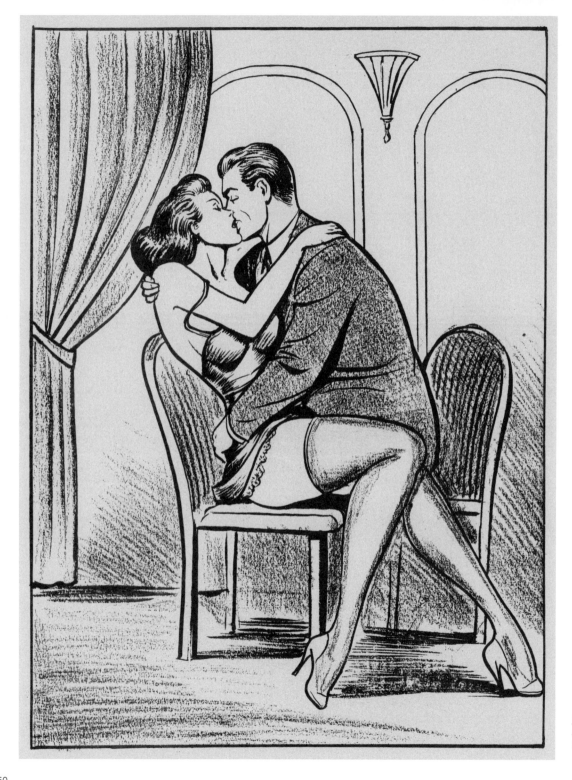

He crushed Lucile's eager body to him, kissed her.

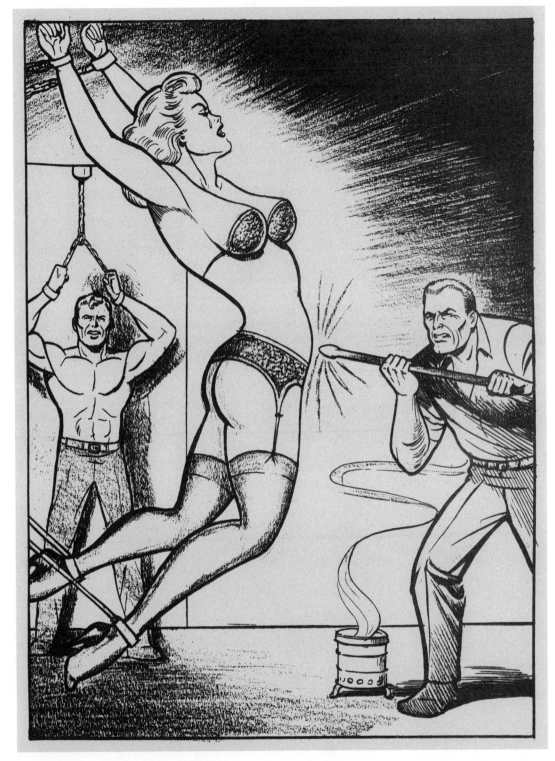

Nina and Jerry screamed at the same time, her slim torso writhered in pain . . .

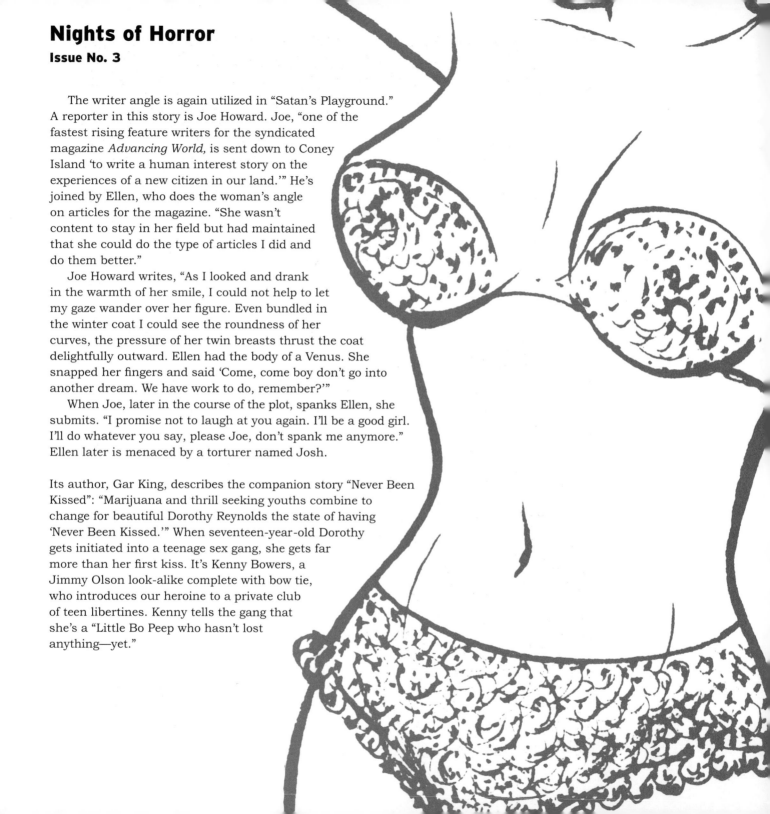

Nights of Horror
Issue No. 3

The writer angle is again utilized in "Satan's Playground." A reporter in this story is Joe Howard. Joe, "one of the fastest rising feature writers for the syndicated magazine *Advancing World,* is sent down to Coney Island 'to write a human interest story on the experiences of a new citizen in our land.'" He's joined by Ellen, who does the woman's angle on articles for the magazine. "She wasn't content to stay in her field but had maintained that she could do the type of articles I did and do them better."

Joe Howard writes, "As I looked and drank in the warmth of her smile, I could not help to let my gaze wander over her figure. Even bundled in the winter coat I could see the roundness of her curves, the pressure of her twin breasts thrust the coat delightfully outward. Ellen had the body of a Venus. She snapped her fingers and said 'Come, come boy don't go into another dream. We have work to do, remember?'"

When Joe, later in the course of the plot, spanks Ellen, she submits. "I promise not to laugh at you again. I'll be a good girl. I'll do whatever you say, please Joe, don't spank me anymore." Ellen later is menaced by a torturer named Josh.

Its author, Gar King, describes the companion story "Never Been Kissed": "Marijuana and thrill seeking youths combine to change for beautiful Dorothy Reynolds the state of having 'Never Been Kissed.'" When seventeen-year-old Dorothy gets initiated into a teenage sex gang, she gets far more than her first kiss. It's Kenny Bowers, a Jimmy Olson look-alike complete with bow tie, who introduces our heroine to a private club of teen libertines. Kenny tells the gang that she's a "Little Bo Peep who hasn't lost anything—yet."

"Satan's Playground"

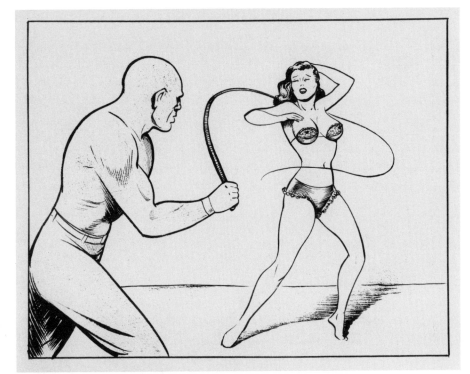

The pageant of the young, white girl, naked, trying to do a lewd dance while a huge, black-as-coal negro chased her about the stage with a whip brought the already inflamed audience to a fever pitch.

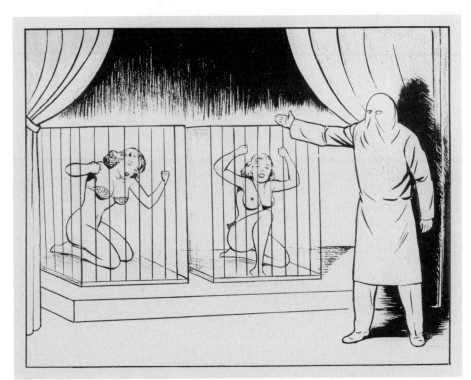

"Open the curtain," he called out. The curtain drew back and revealed to my gaze a sight out of the slave markets of ancient Rome.

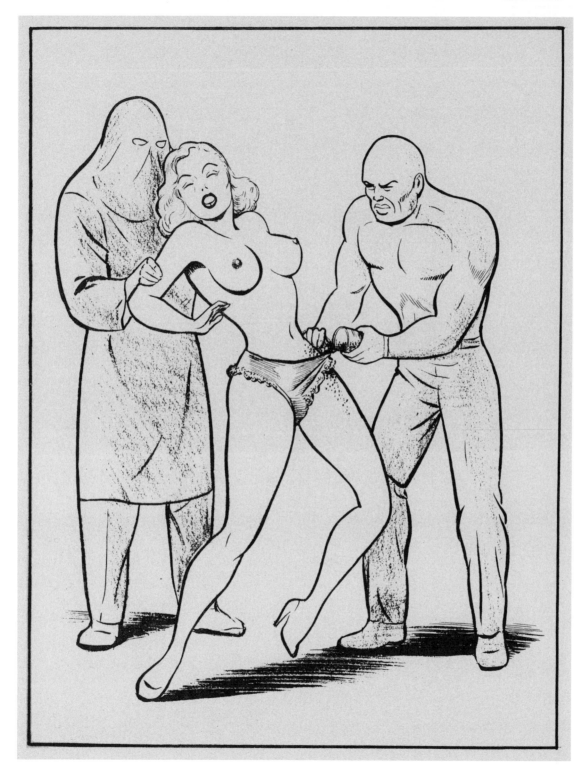

The red ants bit and nipped where the honey had been smeared.

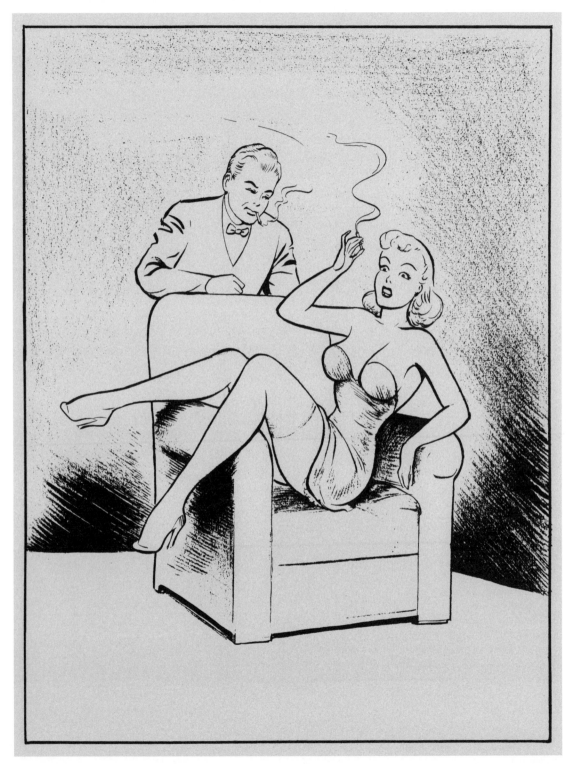

"Puff it in . . . in a few minutes you'll feel wonderful."

(Reefer madness! A Jimmy Olsen look-alike turns a Lucy Lane look-alike on to evil weed.)

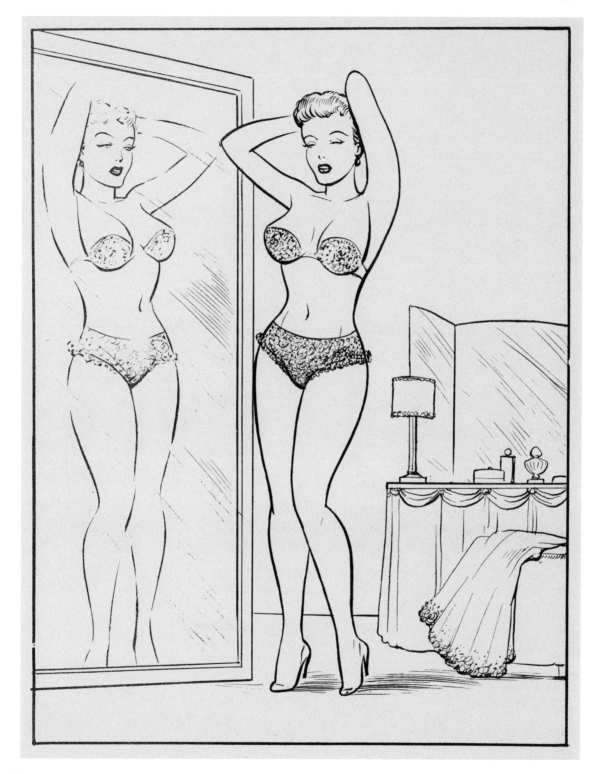

Girls are all bulges and soft.

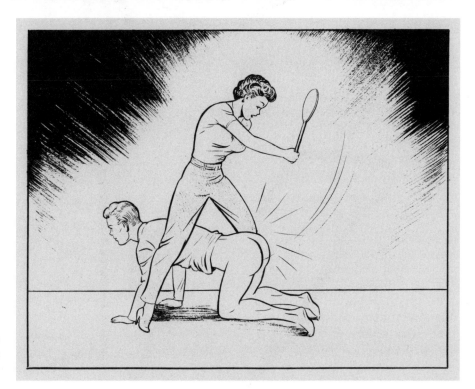

SPLAT! CRACK!
The paddle went in
quick succession.

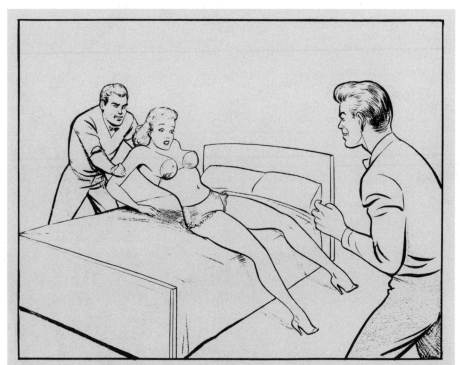

"Lay still, honey, it's
only Rod. He won't
hurt you. He's going
to make you feel
good, just like I did."

57

Nights of Horror
Issue No. 4

The most prolific writer of the series, Gar King, provides a capsule summary of "Girl for Sale": "Because of hardships, Sally Dawson's parents are forced to 'sell' her into marriage with a madman. The strange rites of love he forces Sally to observe are again NIGHTS OF HORROR!" Strange nights, indeed!

The madman Sally's parents sell her to is artist John Bale. Aren't *all* artists "mad," though?

The second half of this book, "Abducted," is again credited to Gar King. This adventure involves a girl, Sally, and her boyfriend, Carl, who kills her sadistic kidnapper, John Bale. Carl gets off a murder rap thanks to a "lawyer he had met in the service and who came to the aid of a friend when he needed help. But perhaps that is another story." Perhaps it is.

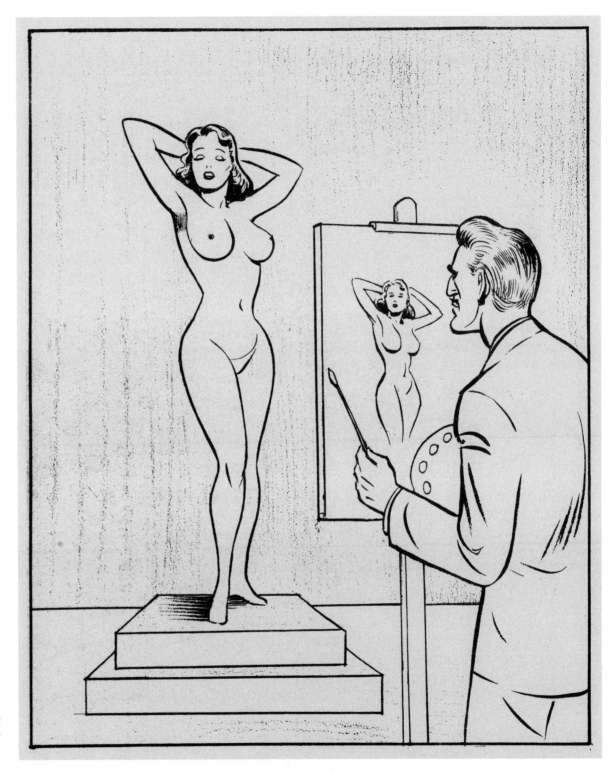

"Girl for Sale"

At last he had her posed to his satisfaction.

59

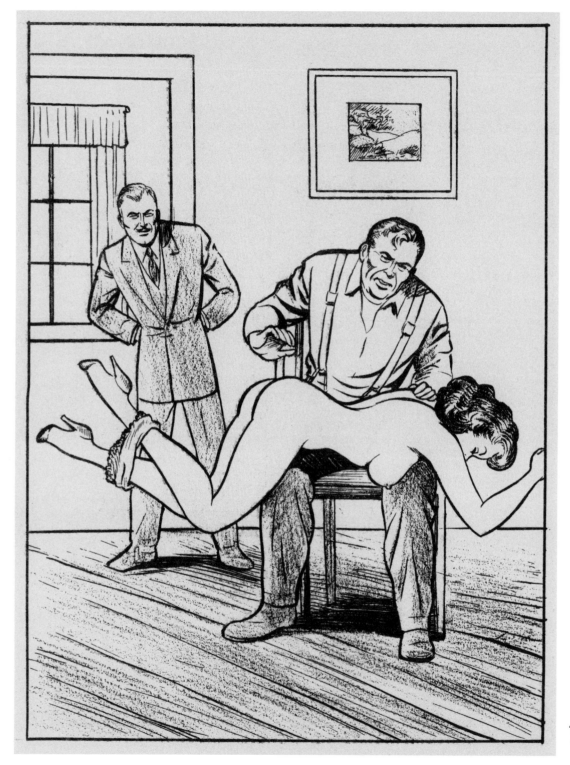

"Please stop! I'll do as you say!"

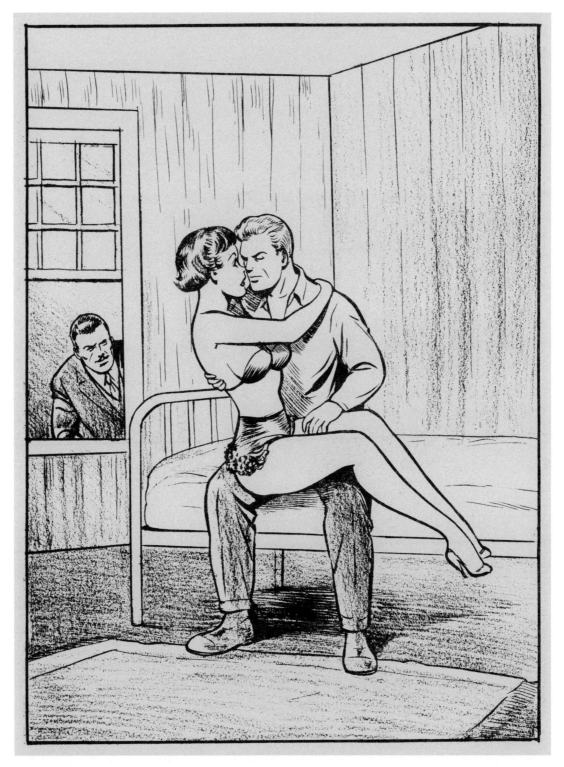

*She did his
bidding, so that
he could take
perverse pleasure
from watching.*

"Abducted"

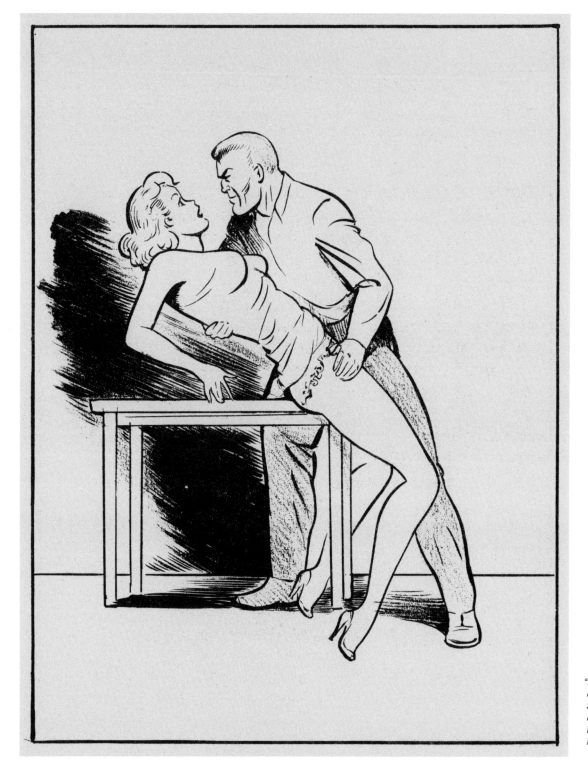

*"Please, Jake
didn't go that high."
She reached down
and drew her slip
back to where it
had been.*

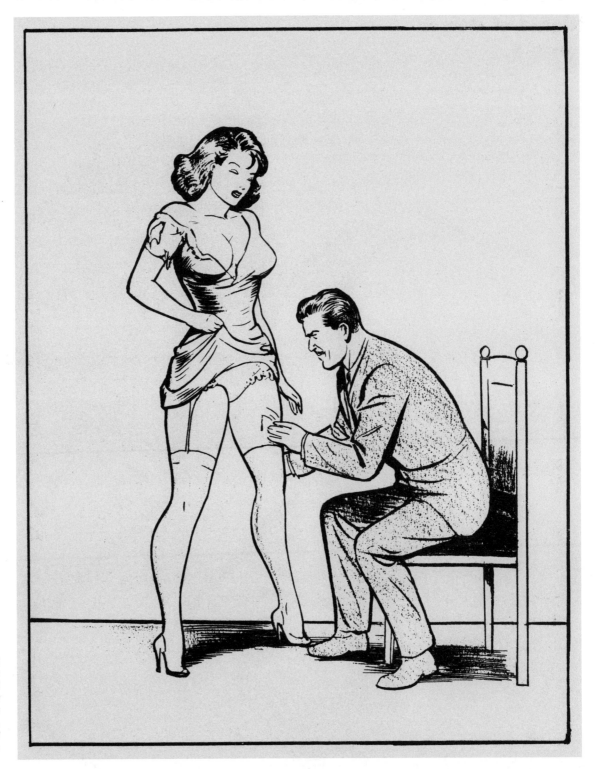

Her pleas seemed
only to infuriate
Jake. He stopped
his soft squeezing
and dug his nails
into her thigh,
causing Judy to cry
out in pain.

Nights of Horror
Issue No. 5

In this story by Gavin Moore, "The Vortex," we learn on the first page that Anne Miller "thought her luckiest break had been acquiring Claire Williams for her roommate." A lucky break, too, for readers of *Nights of Horror,* who maybe never imagined the fascination of Sappho love. But this book-length tale gets more complicated than that, as stories in this series always do.

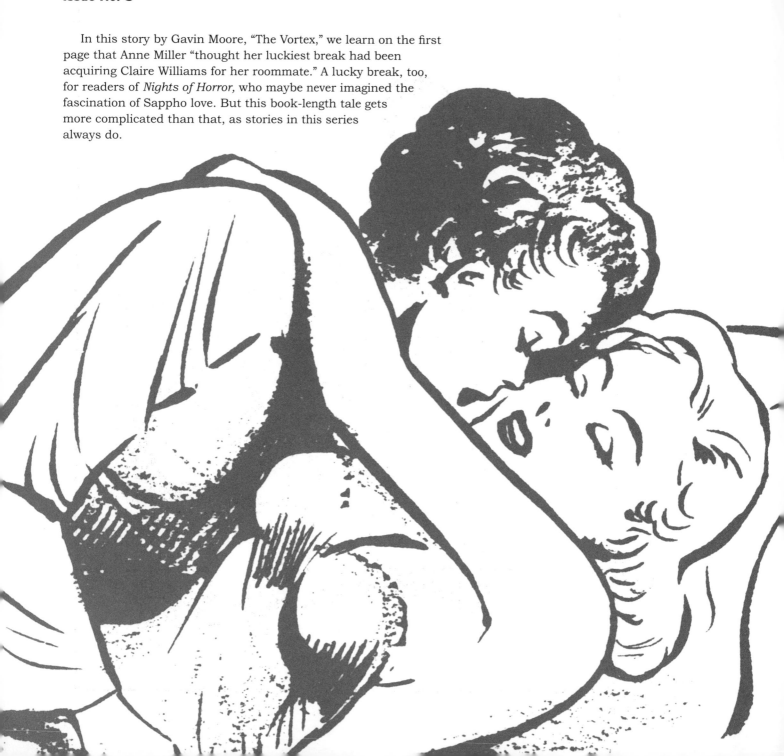

"The Vortex"

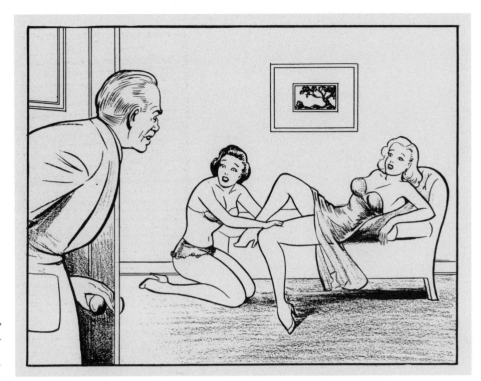

"What is the meaning of this?" he said, simulating in his voice cold anger.

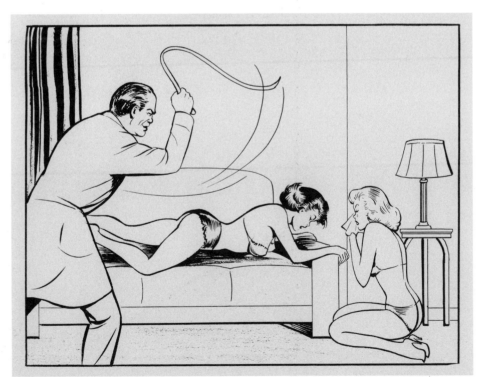

He brought the lash down with a whistling thud across the roundness of Claire.

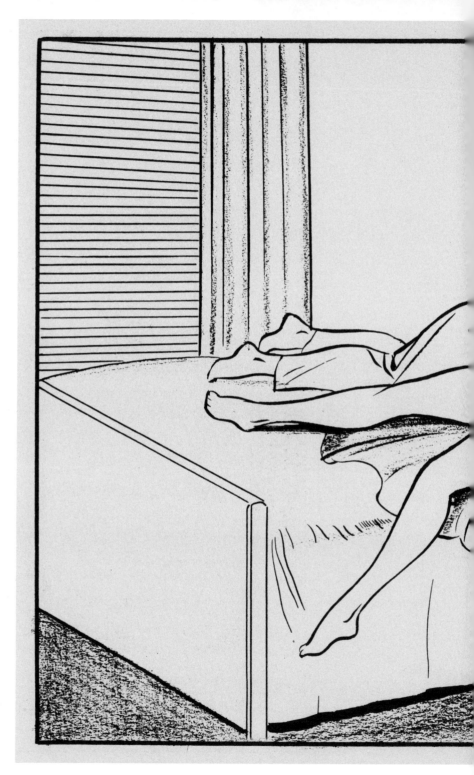

Anne squirmed at the thrill that coursed through her.

*"Oh-Oh-Jerry—
don't—"*

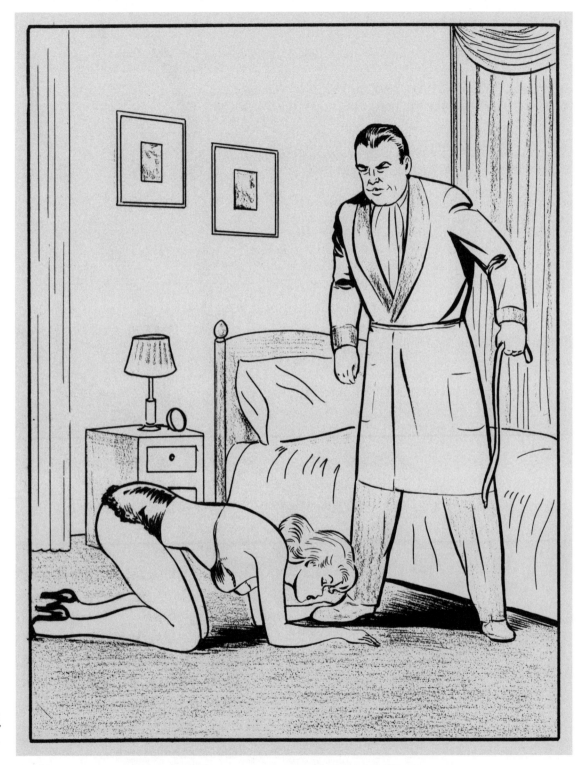

"Implant upon my foot your most servile caress," he ordered.

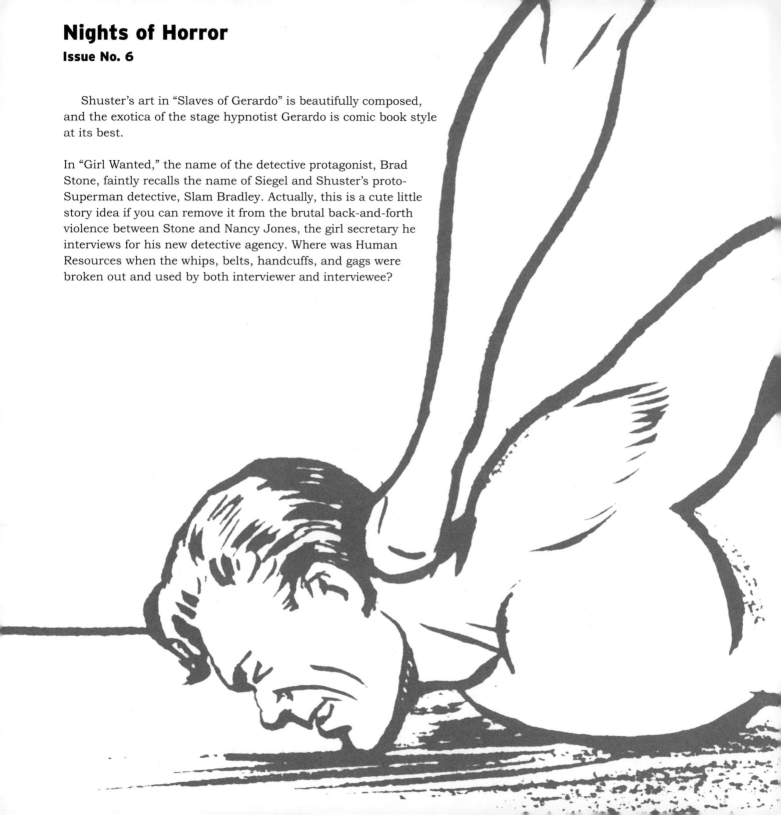

Nights of Horror
Issue No. 6

Shuster's art in "Slaves of Gerardo" is beautifully composed, and the exotica of the stage hypnotist Gerardo is comic book style at its best.

In "Girl Wanted," the name of the detective protagonist, Brad Stone, faintly recalls the name of Siegel and Shuster's proto-Superman detective, Slam Bradley. Actually, this is a cute little story idea if you can remove it from the brutal back-and-forth violence between Stone and Nancy Jones, the girl secretary he interviews for his new detective agency. Where was Human Resources when the whips, belts, handcuffs, and gags were broken out and used by both interviewer and interviewee?

"Slaves of Gerardo"

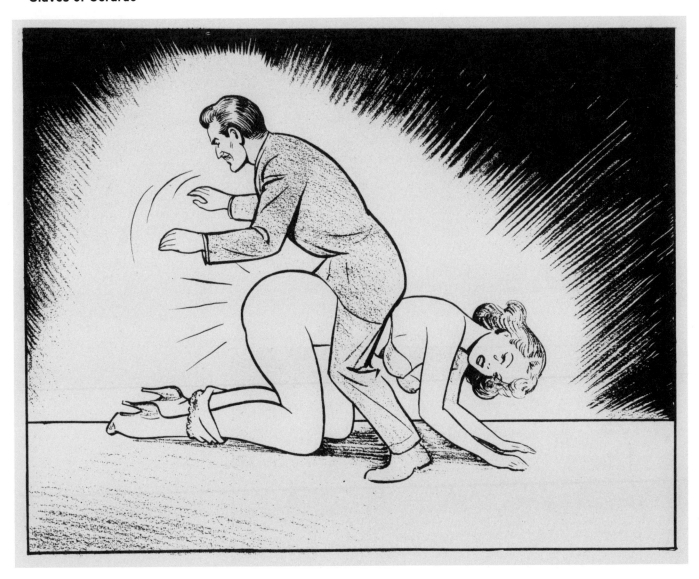

*With both hands he slapped and
cuffed the soft whiteness.*

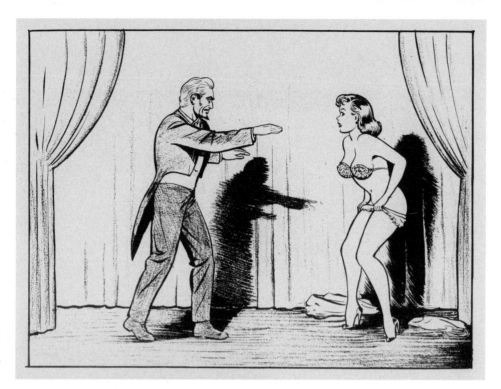

*Gerardo gestured,
"You are Fifi
La Tour, a strip
tease dancer."*

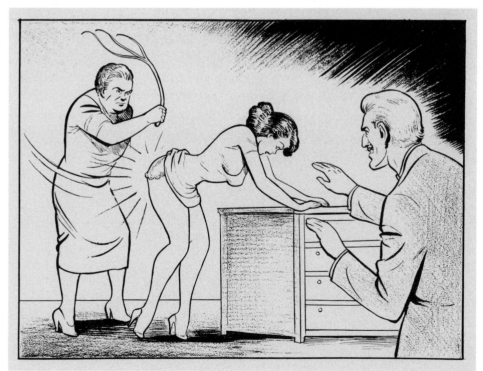

*"You are my
slave; my will
is your will."*

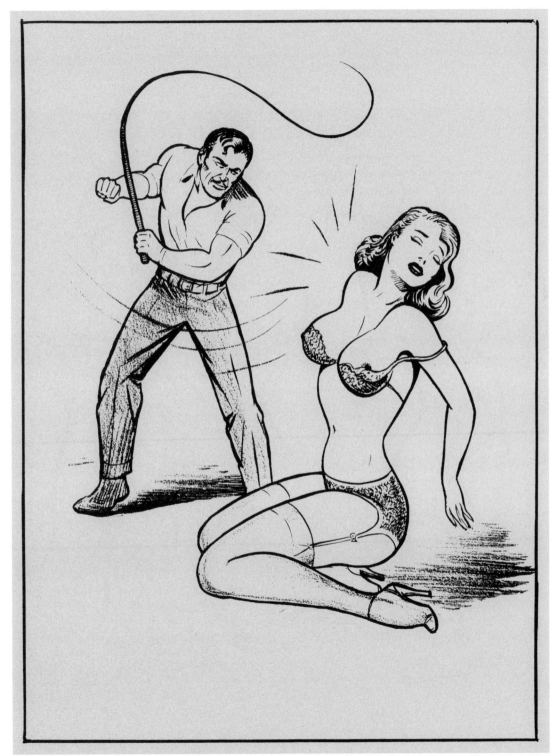

"You're mine, all mine, you witch."

(This image was Exhibit 3 in the April 1955 Senate hearings on "Pornography and its Effects on Juvenile Delinquency.")

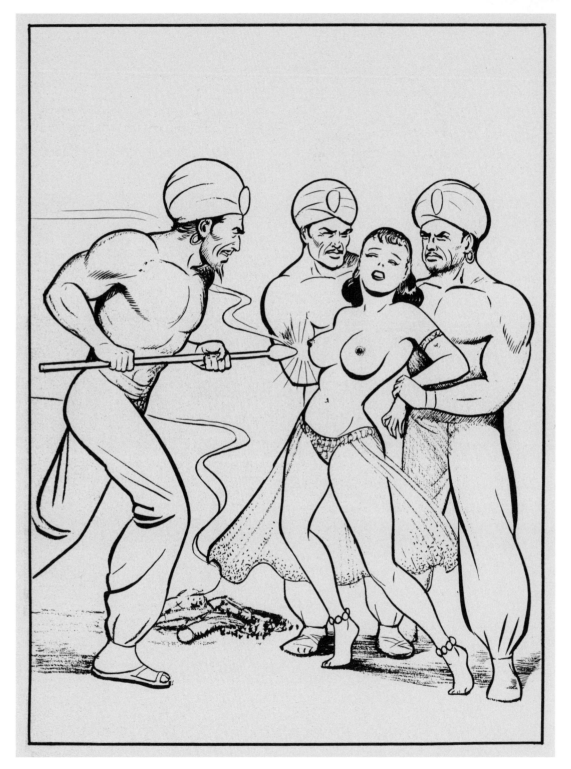

The white hot iron was pointed towards her—

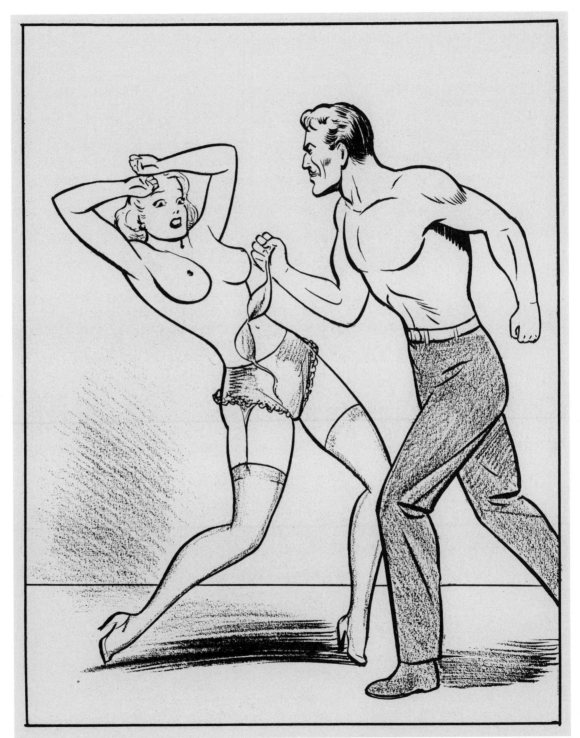

"I'll teach you not to go out with someone else!"

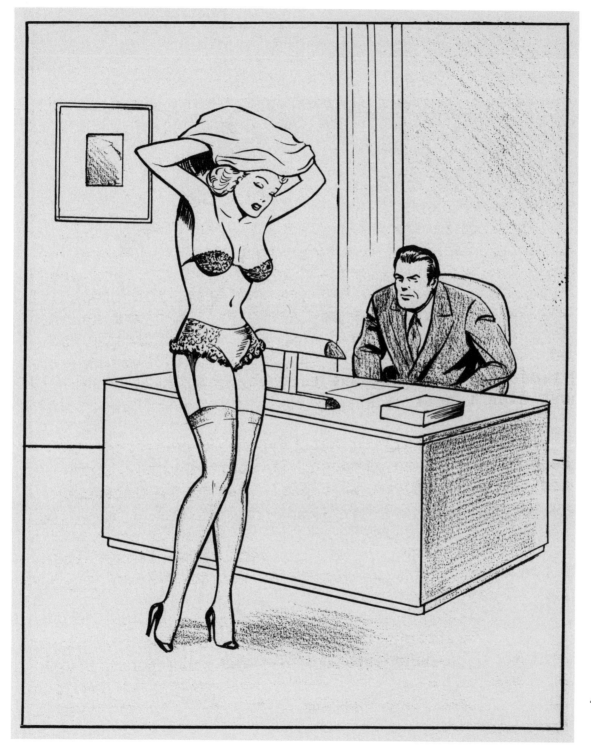

"Girl Wanted"

"I'll be what you want . . . if you let me have the job."

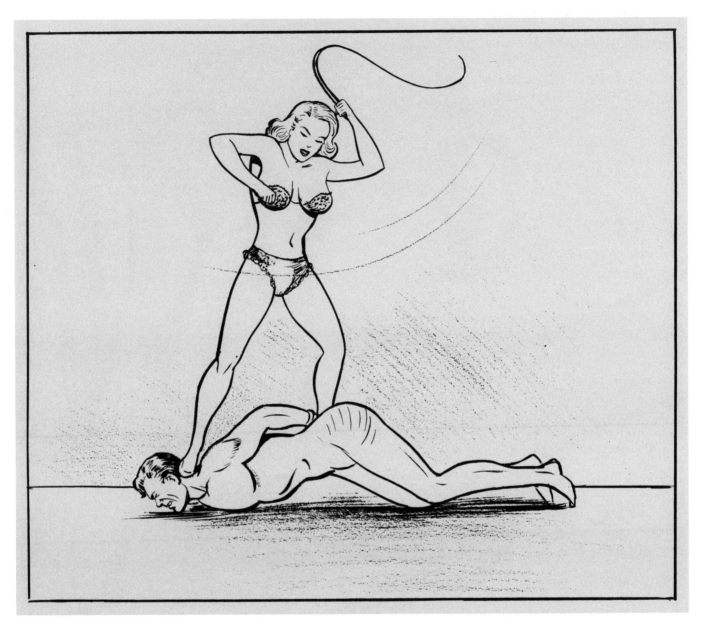

"How do you like this—and this!"

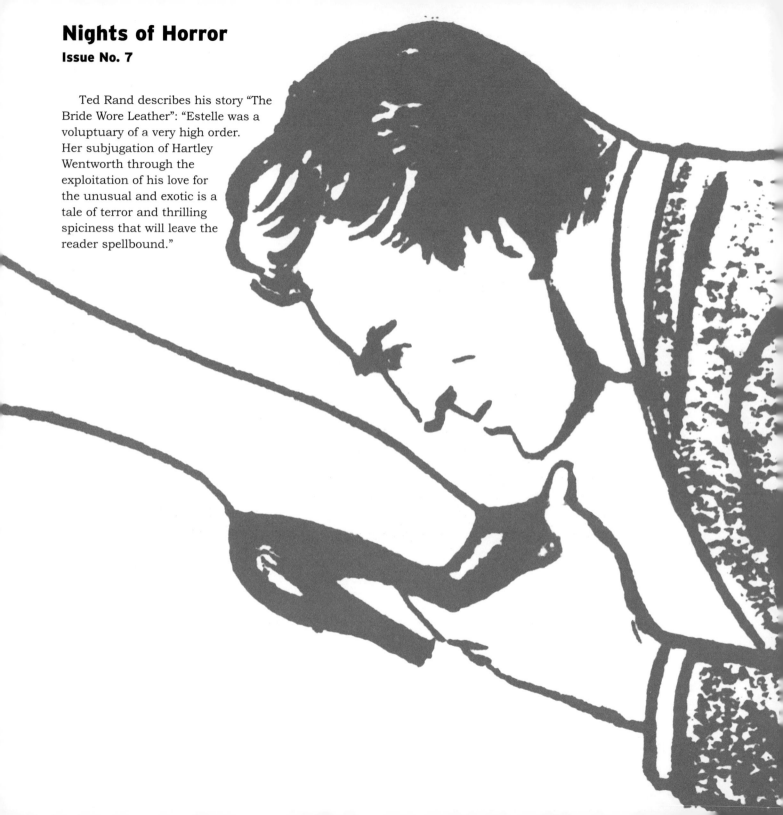

Nights of Horror
Issue No. 7

Ted Rand describes his story "The Bride Wore Leather": "Estelle was a voluptuary of a very high order. Her subjugation of Hartley Wentworth through the exploitation of his love for the unusual and exotic is a tale of terror and thrilling spiciness that will leave the reader spellbound."

"The Bride Wore Leather"

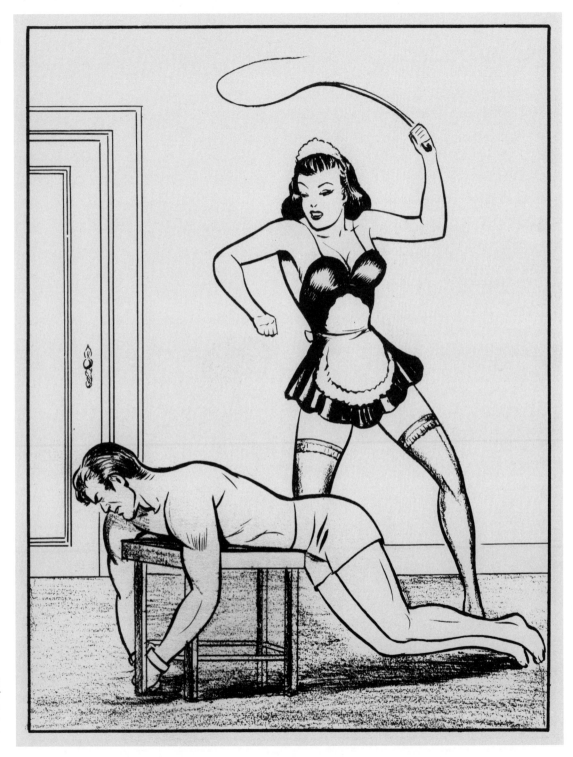

The whip fell relentlessly as if Etty were embued with the same fervor as her mistress.

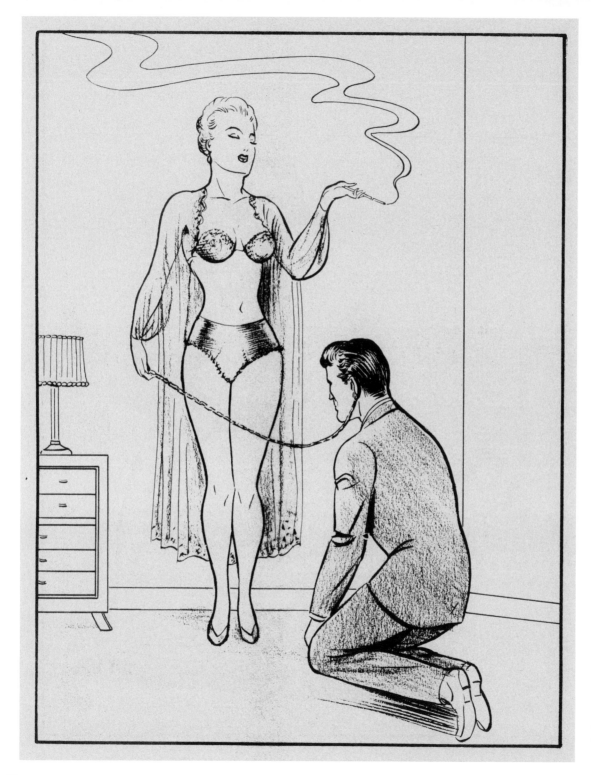

Estelle led him further and further up the road to slavery.

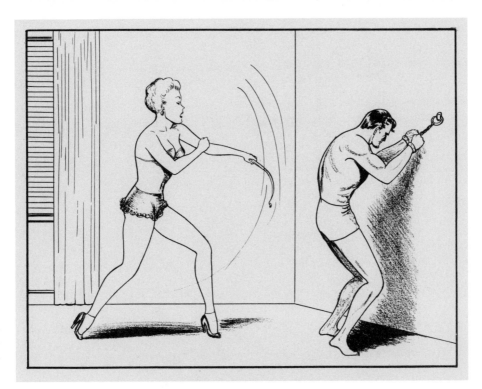

THWACK! The sound of the blow resounded in the room.

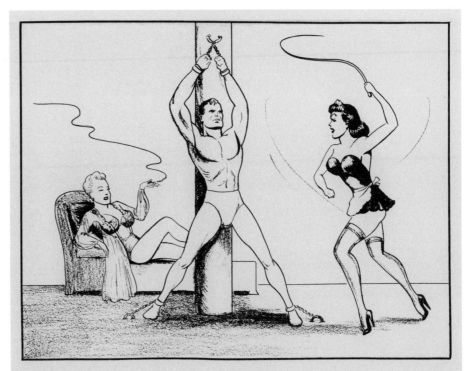

Estelle, by sign, indicated that she wished to have the maid continue.

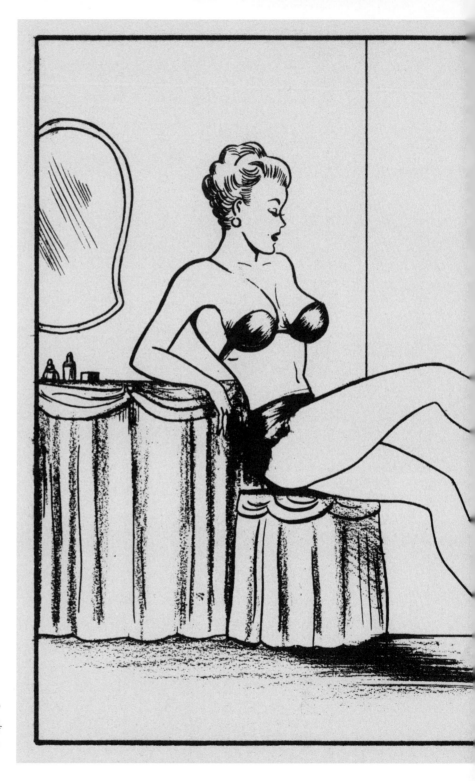

He proceeded to lave, slavishly, the sole of Estelle's boot.

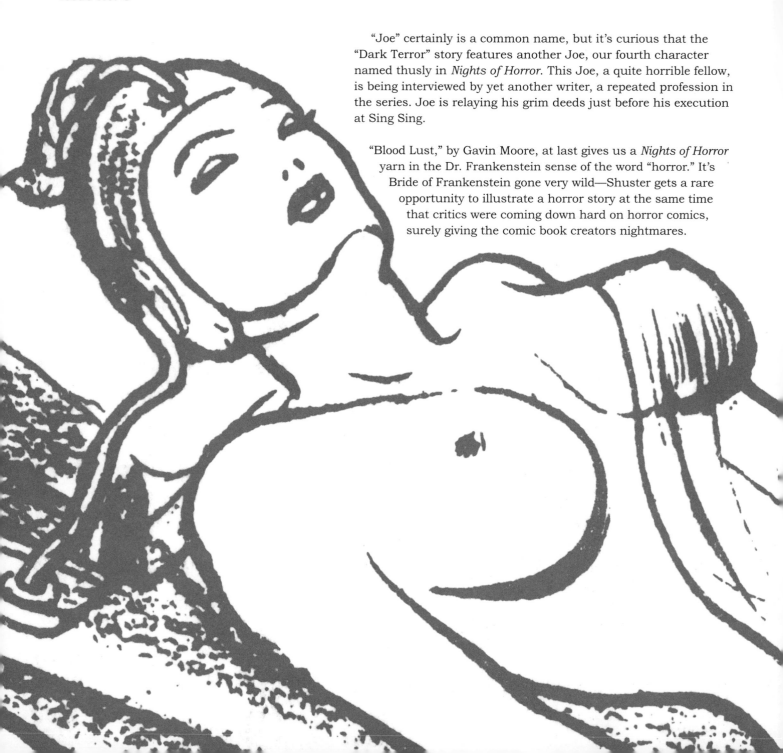

Nights of Horror
Issue No. 8

"Joe" certainly is a common name, but it's curious that the "Dark Terror" story features another Joe, our fourth character named thusly in *Nights of Horror*. This Joe, a quite horrible fellow, is being interviewed by yet another writer, a repeated profession in the series. Joe is relaying his grim deeds just before his execution at Sing Sing.

"Blood Lust," by Gavin Moore, at last gives us a *Nights of Horror* yarn in the Dr. Frankenstein sense of the word "horror." It's Bride of Frankenstein gone very wild—Shuster gets a rare opportunity to illustrate a horror story at the same time that critics were coming down hard on horror comics, surely giving the comic book creators nightmares.

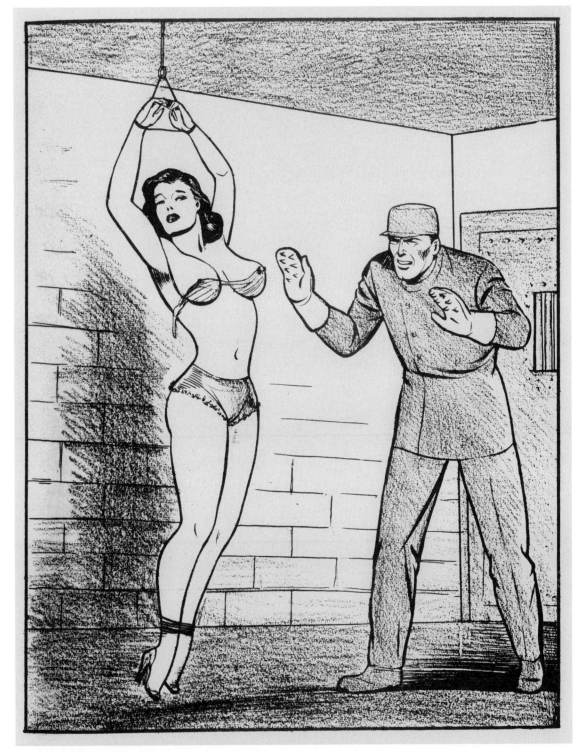

"Dark Terror"

He started for her, his leering eyes devouring her shrinking form.

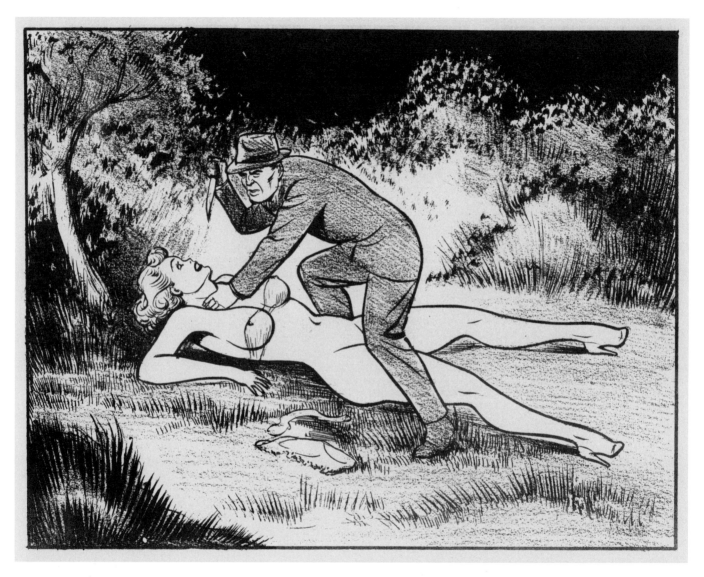

*The knife flashed as her opened
mouth emitted a scream.*

"Blood Lust"

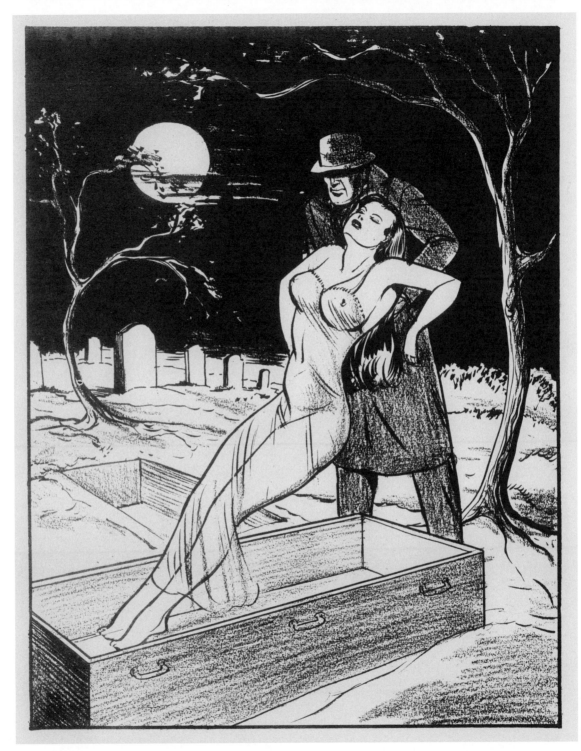

*The furtive figure
wrestled the corpse
from the coffin.*

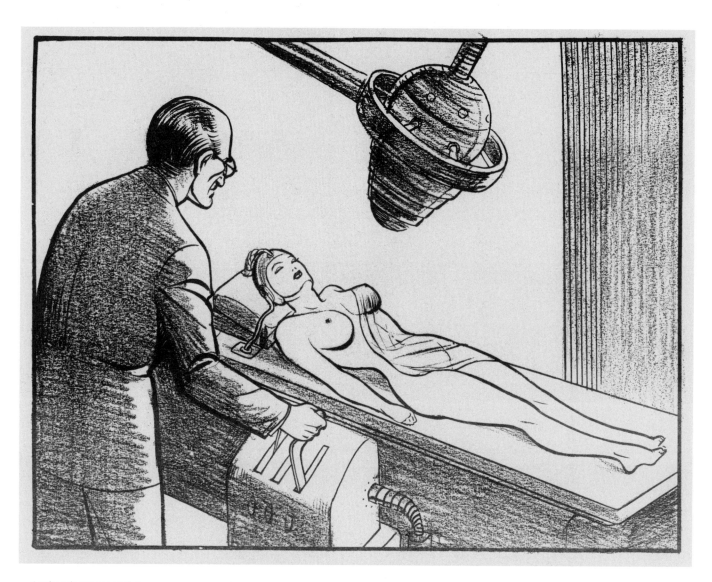

*As the minutes passed, he
detected a faint pulse of life.*

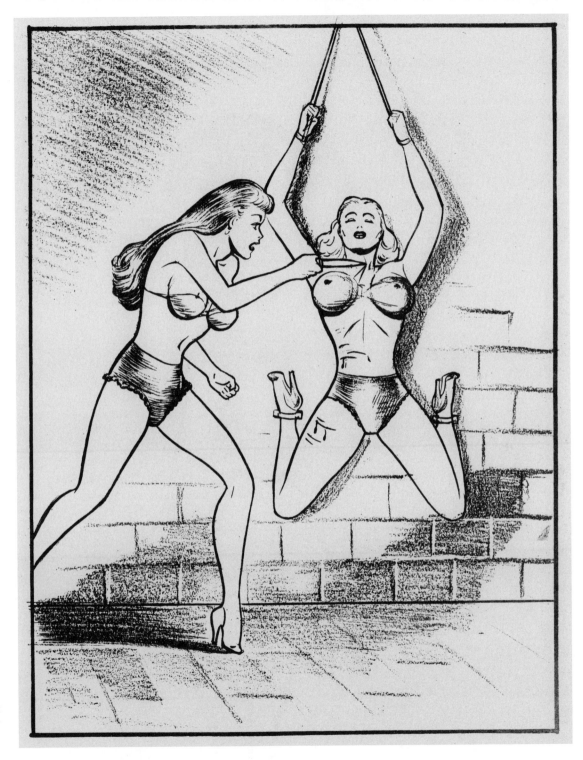

Her blood lust at a peak, she directed the blade towards the throat.

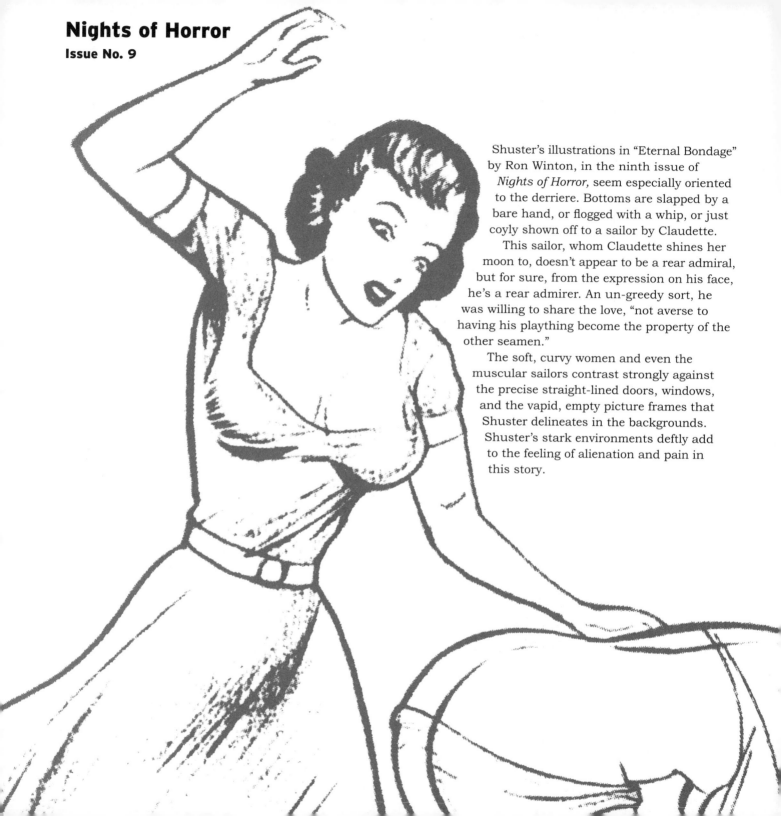

Shuster's illustrations in "Eternal Bondage" by Ron Winton, in the ninth issue of *Nights of Horror,* seem especially oriented to the derriere. Bottoms are slapped by a bare hand, or flogged with a whip, or just coyly shown off to a sailor by Claudette.

This sailor, whom Claudette shines her moon to, doesn't appear to be a rear admiral, but for sure, from the expression on his face, he's a rear admirer. An un-greedy sort, he was willing to share the love, "not averse to having his plaything become the property of the other seamen."

The soft, curvy women and even the muscular sailors contrast strongly against the precise straight-lined doors, windows, and the vapid, empty picture frames that Shuster delineates in the backgrounds. Shuster's stark environments deftly add to the feeling of alienation and pain in this story.

"Eternal Bondage"

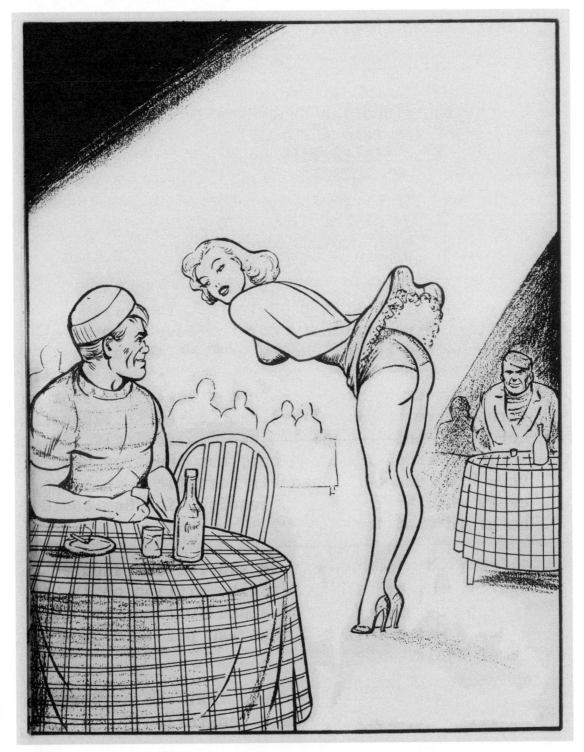

Imitating a dancer,
Claudette flipped
her skirt and
exposed herself.

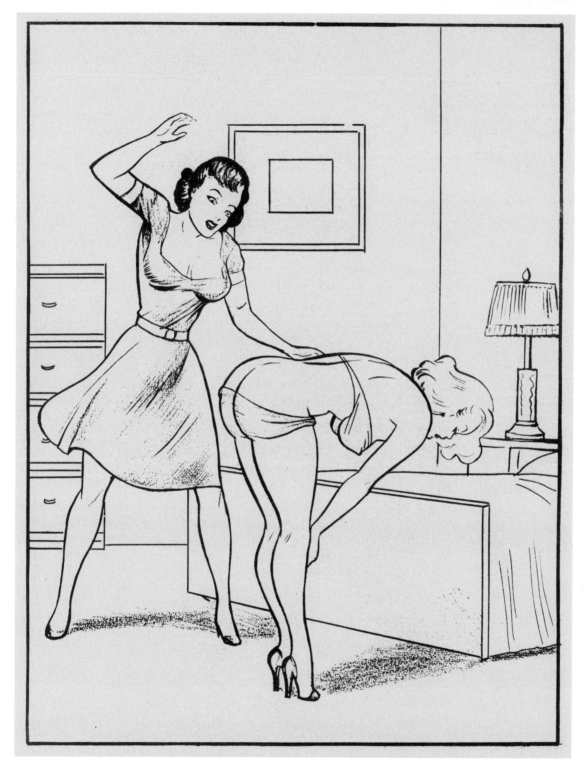

"Harder," she murmured, shivering with excitement.

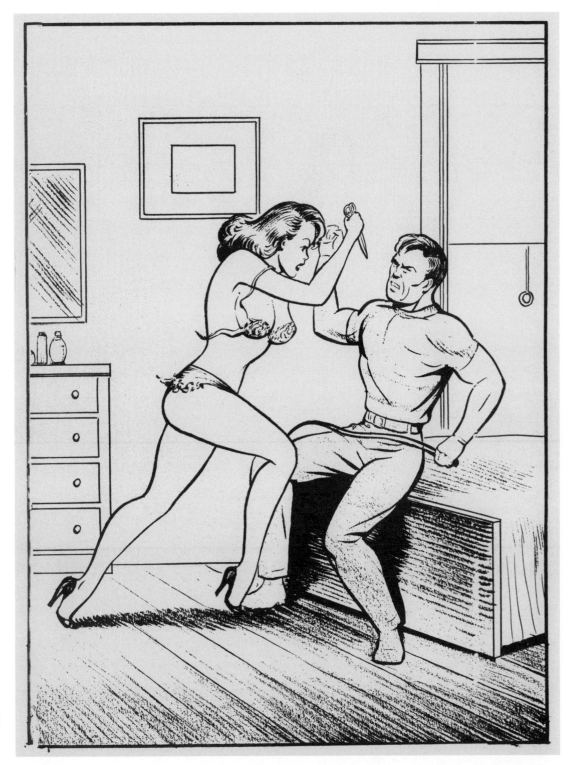

*In desperation
she grasped
the instrument
and menaced
Baroque with it.*

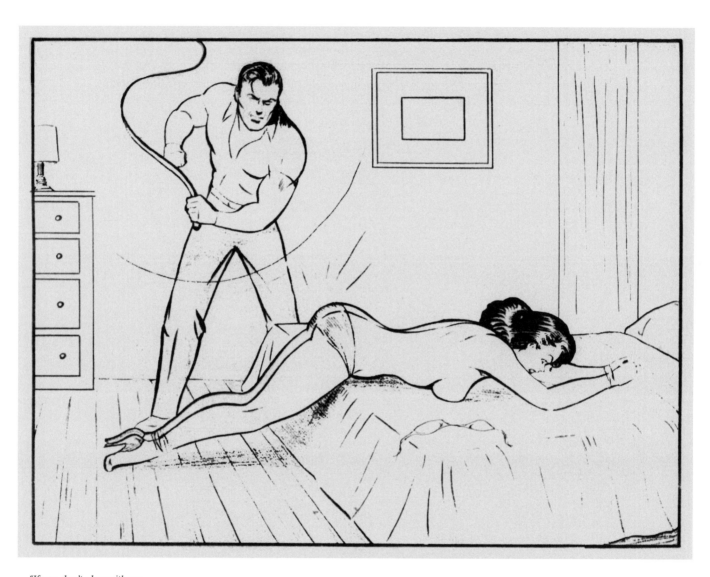

"If you don't play with me willingly—I'll have some fun with you without your consent."

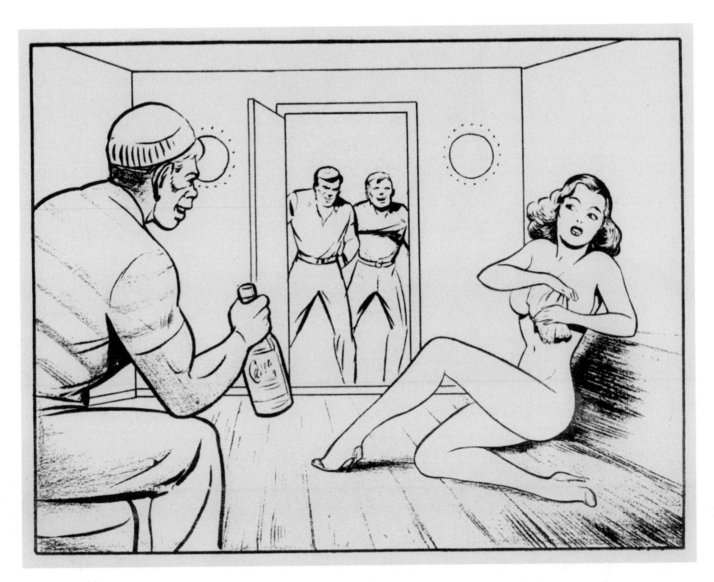

He was not averse to having his plaything become the property of the other seamen.

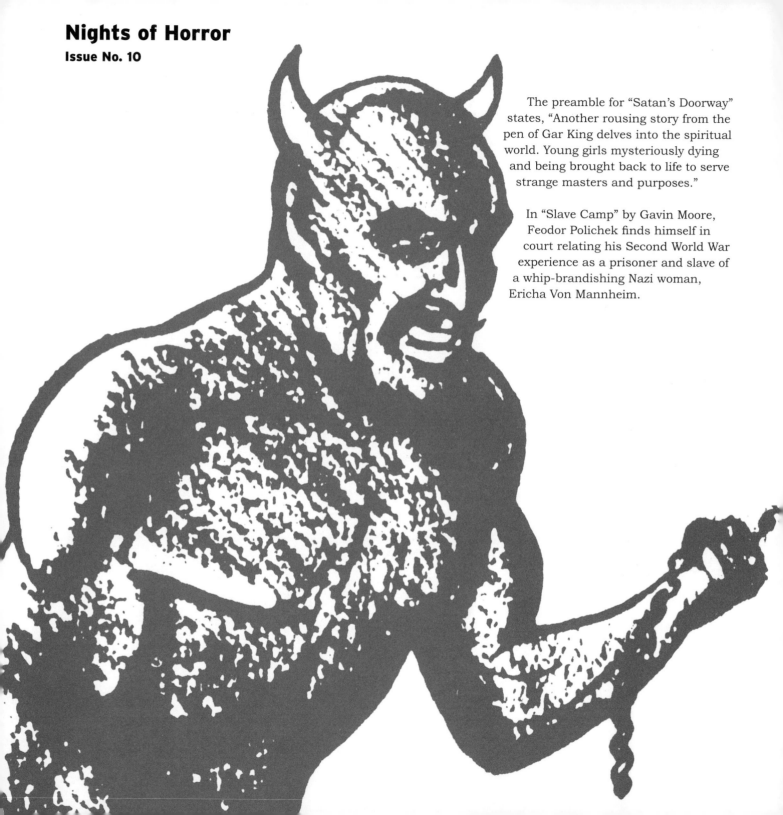

Nights of Horror
Issue No. 10

The preamble for "Satan's Doorway" states, "Another rousing story from the pen of Gar King delves into the spiritual world. Young girls mysteriously dying and being brought back to life to serve strange masters and purposes."

In "Slave Camp" by Gavin Moore, Feodor Polichek finds himself in court relating his Second World War experience as a prisoner and slave of a whip-brandishing Nazi woman, Ericha Von Mannheim.

"Satan's Doorway"

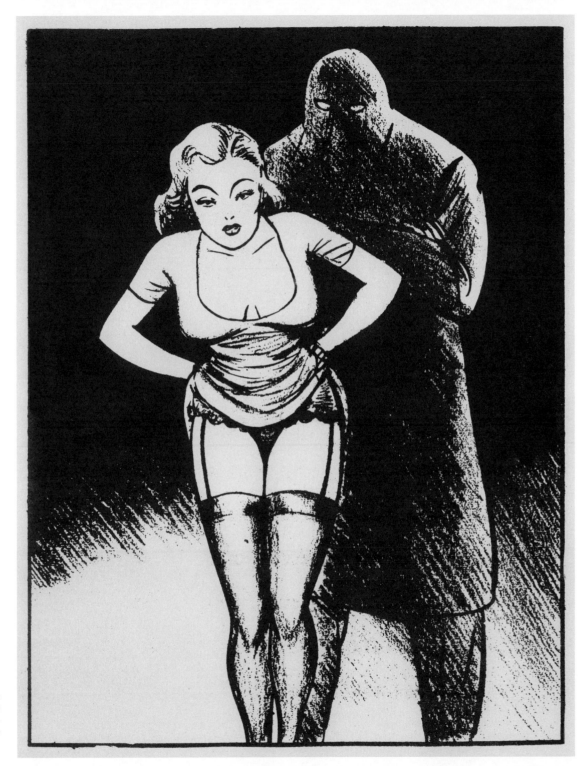

Jean followed his commands with no shame or realization of what she was doing.

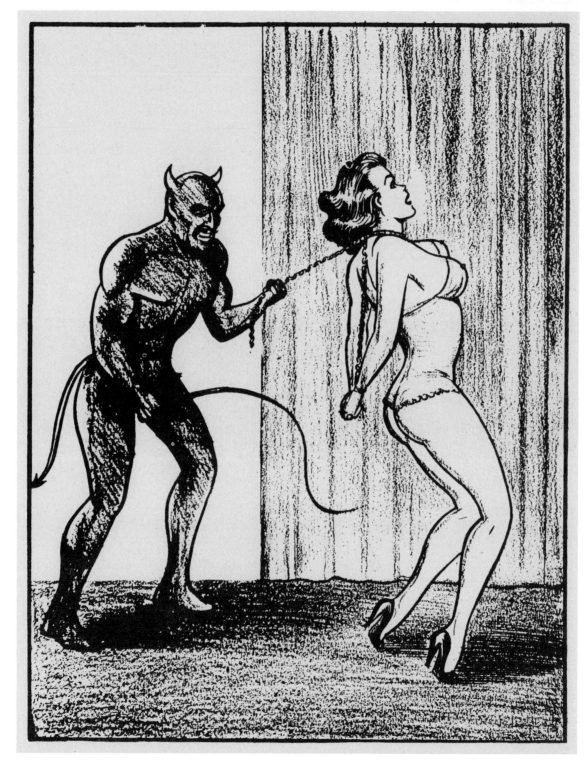

Her plantive cries
came. "Please—no
more, I'll be good."

(This image was
Exhibit 2 in the
April 1955 Senate
hearings on
"Pornography
and its Effects
on Juvenile
Delinquency.")

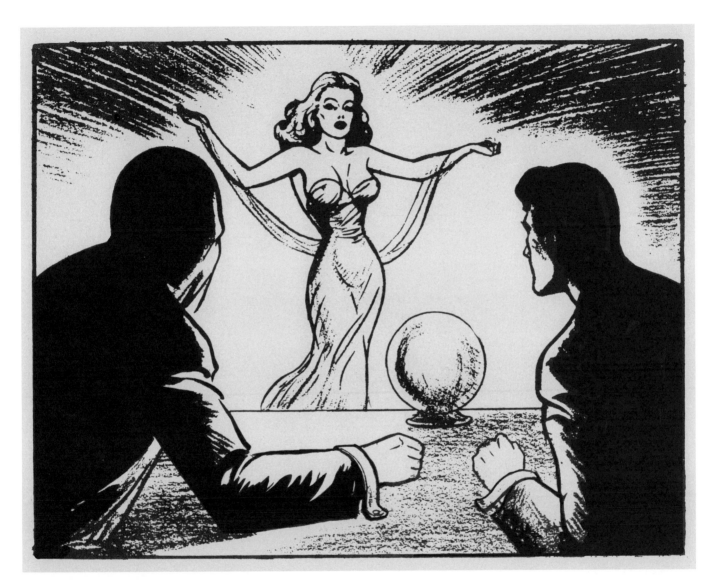

I knew she was well built, but I
never imagined she had the
lucious body I saw that night.

"Slave Camp"

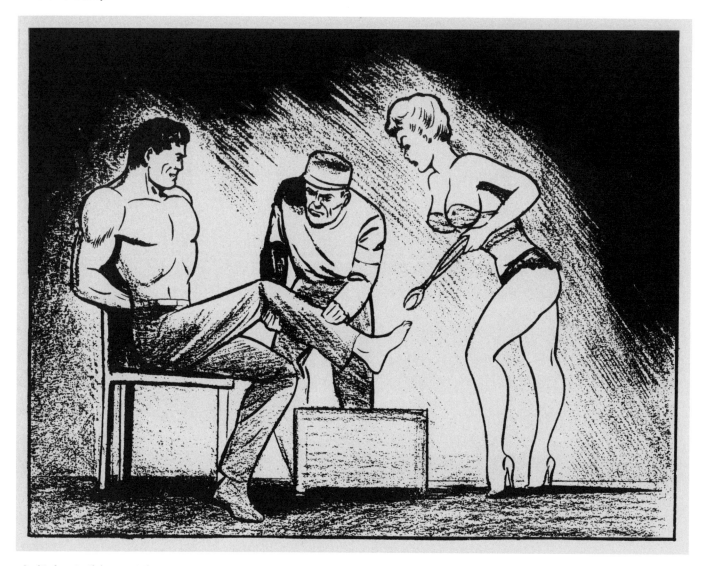

I gritted my teeth in expectation of the coming ordeal.

(This image was Exhibit 4 in the April 1955 Senate hearings on "Pornography and its Effects on Juvenile Delinquency.")

My stubborn silence only goaded Ericha all the more.

She wanted me for her servant—her slave.

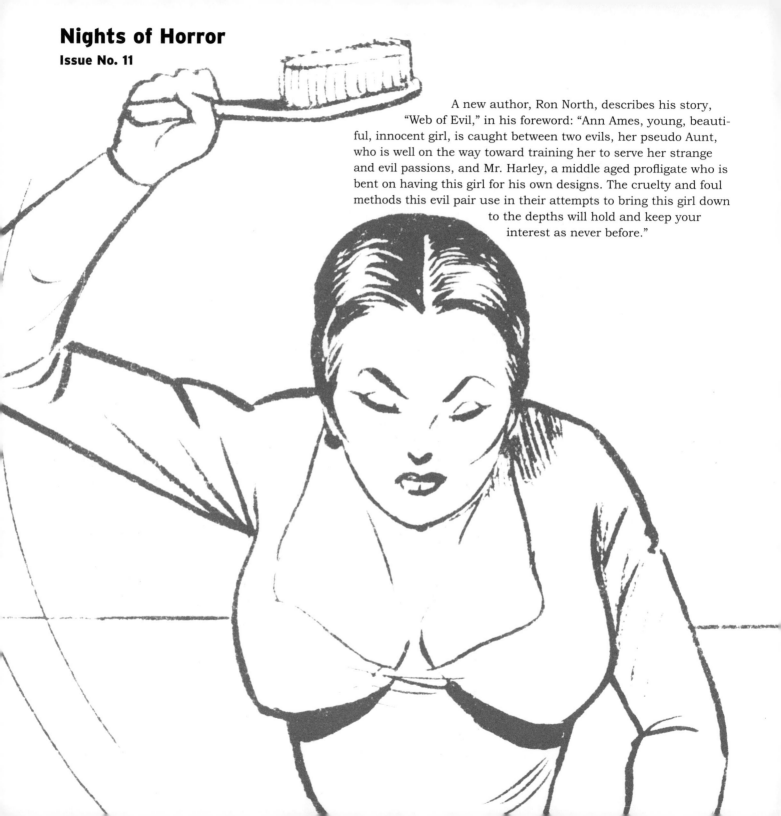

A new author, Ron North, describes his story, "Web of Evil," in his foreword: "Ann Ames, young, beautiful, innocent girl, is caught between two evils, her pseudo Aunt, who is well on the way toward training her to serve her strange and evil passions, and Mr. Harley, a middle aged profligate who is bent on having this girl for his own designs. The cruelty and foul methods this evil pair use in their attempts to bring this girl down to the depths will hold and keep your interest as never before."

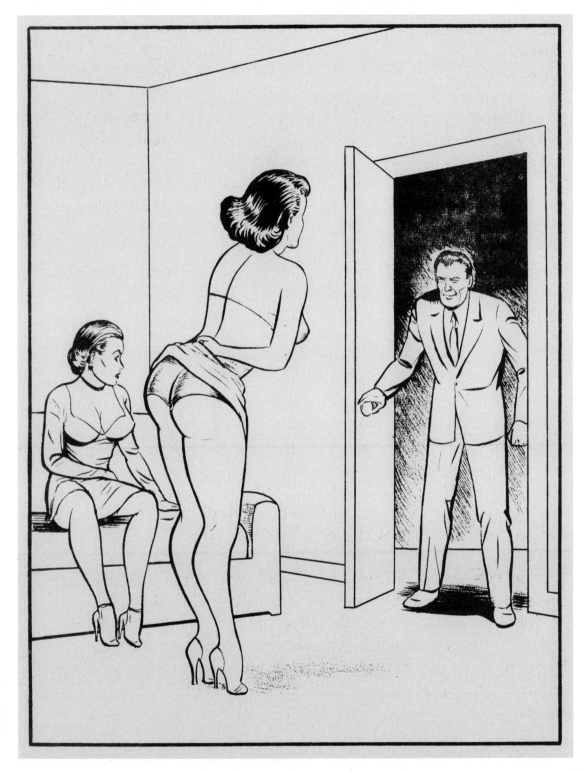

*Ann, her dress
still up, faced
the unexpected
intruder.*

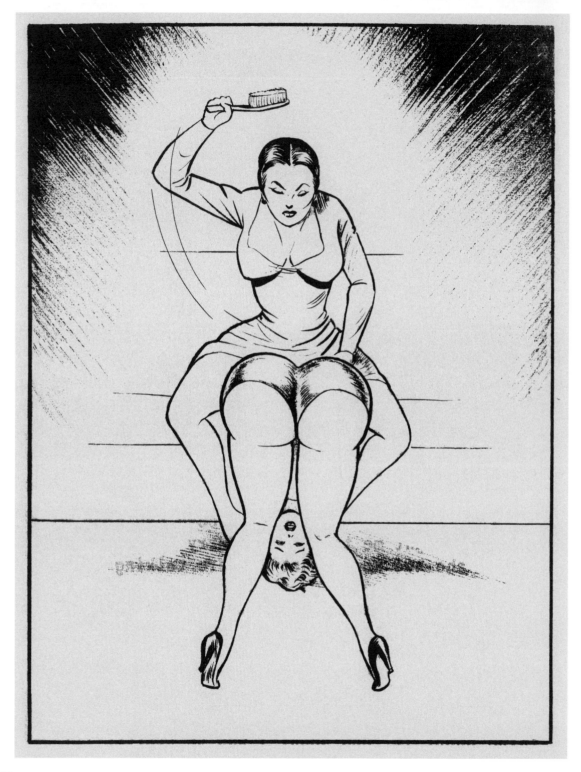

*Aunt Irene's evil
passion took many
and varied forms.*

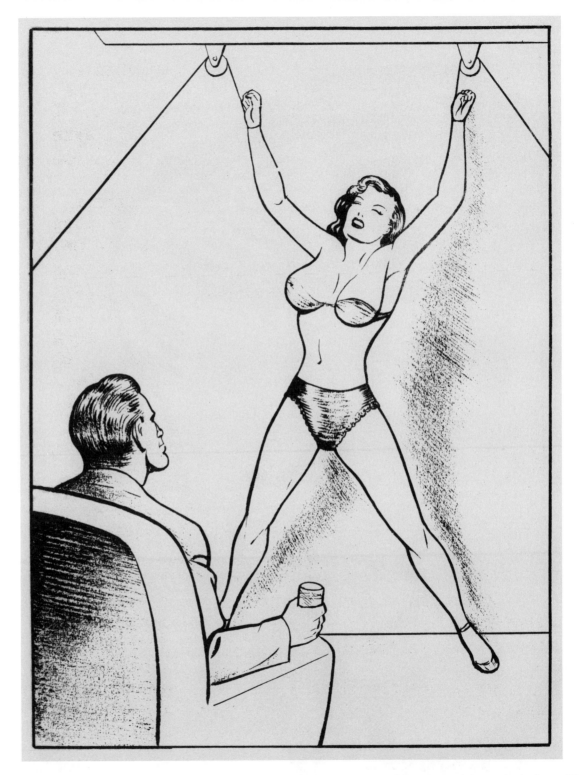

Harley gloated at
Ann's agony.

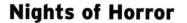

The main figure in "Man and Beast" is yet another writer. This one is Kenneth Baines. In this story, we learn about Baines's career: "The only things he had written up until now had been a series of children's stories that had a quaint charm and appeal to them and they had sold moderately well. With the assurance and confidence that he had gained from the publication of these he had gotten the idea that he wanted to branch out and do something else. He figured his best opportunity would be to write for pulp for awhile . . ." Could this echo somebody we know?

Who says that the *Nights of Horror* booklets didn't do their part to curb juvenile delinquency? In "The Initiation," Johnny Williams is lured into a teenage sex cult. His initiation entails having his bare bottom caned by one of the female members as the others look on. When the cult gets drunk, they welcome older men who start pawing the girls' "delicious" breasts. Johnny gets fed up and goes to the police. The men are sent to the penitentiary and the kids to a correctional institute. Johnny joins the Police Athletic League and becomes one of its star athletes.

The story ends with the stirring moral: "Thus, a hotbed of juvenile delinquency and vice was eradicated, and a young boy who might have been influenced into a life of crime, was instead rescued from his evil associates and started well on the way toward becoming a useful and law-abiding citizen."

"Man and Beast"

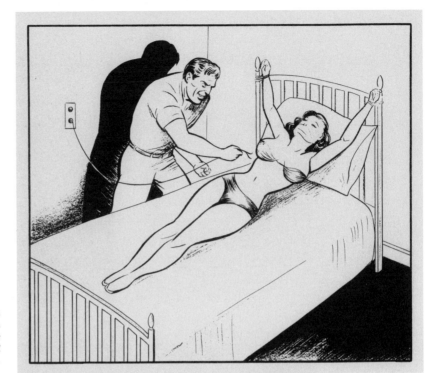

Her body arched in
a tortured leap from
the bed as the
current surged
through her.

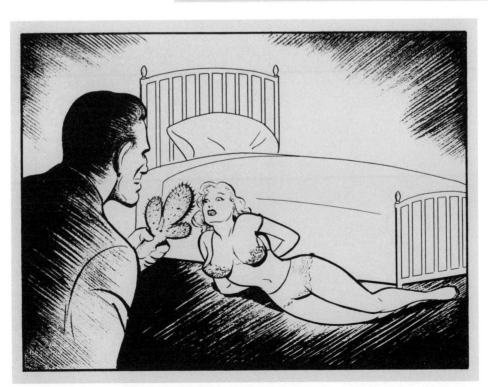

I began to pat it on
the naked skin of
the lush beauty
beneath me.

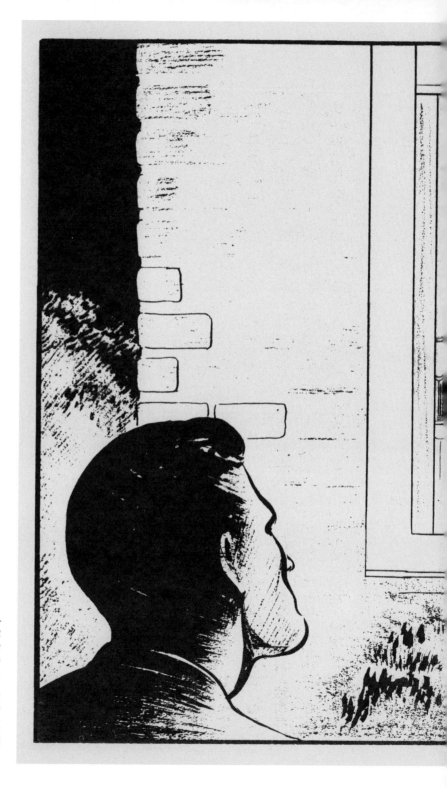

She drew off her lovely, lace-edged slip and stood there gloriously alive in her semi-nudity.

(S&M wasn't the only perversion show in Nights of Horror. *Voyeurism was a recurring motif.)*

"The Initiation"

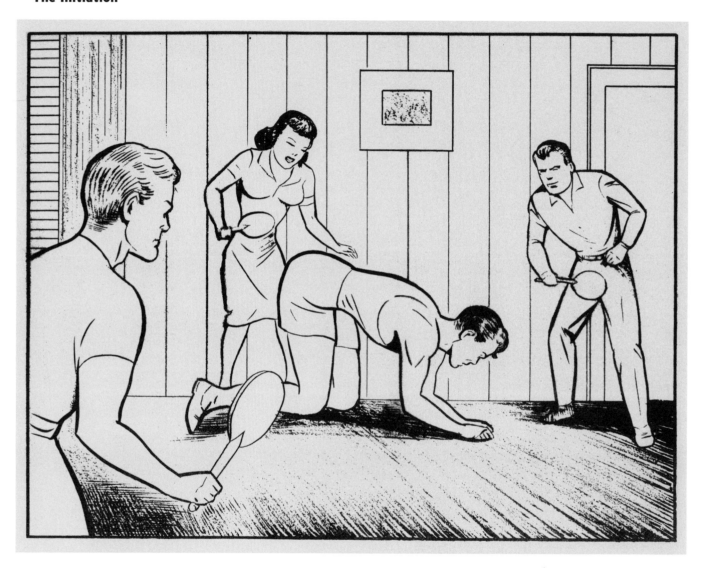

As each blow landed, a livid, red
welp sprang across his rump.

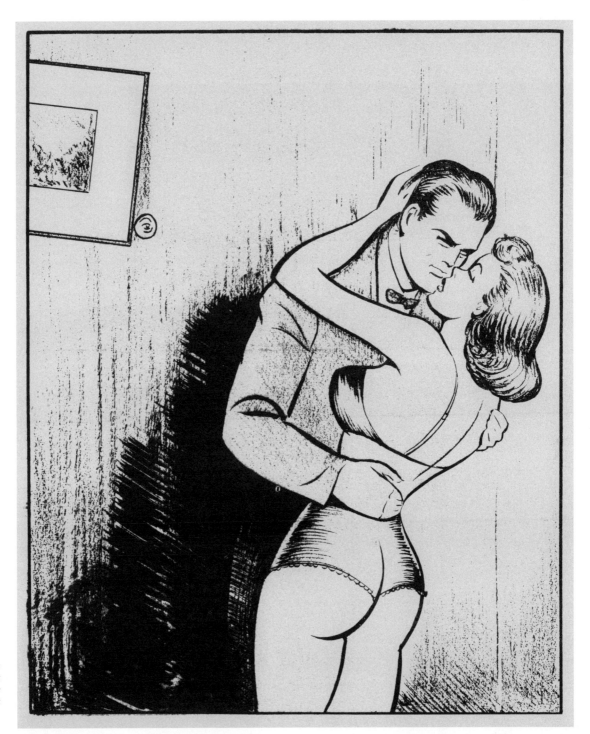

The old lecher's eyes widened at the peephole as he watched what followed.

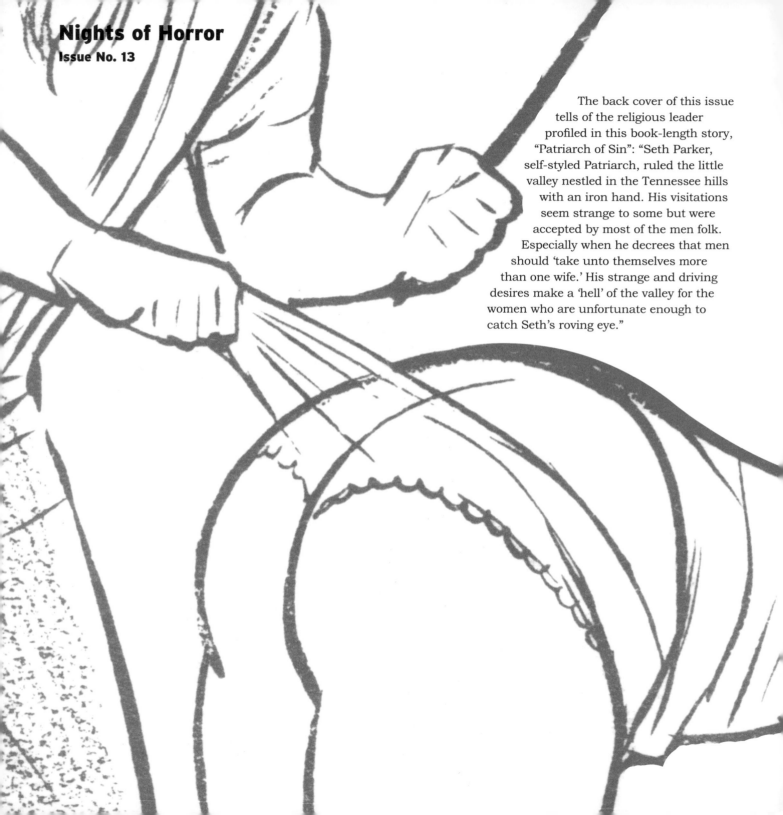

Nights of Horror
Issue No. 13

The back cover of this issue tells of the religious leader profiled in this book-length story, "Patriarch of Sin": "Seth Parker, self-styled Patriarch, ruled the little valley nestled in the Tennessee hills with an iron hand. His visitations seem strange to some but were accepted by most of the men folk. Especially when he decrees that men should 'take unto themselves more than one wife.' His strange and driving desires make a 'hell' of the valley for the women who are unfortunate enough to catch Seth's roving eye."

"Patriarch of Sin"

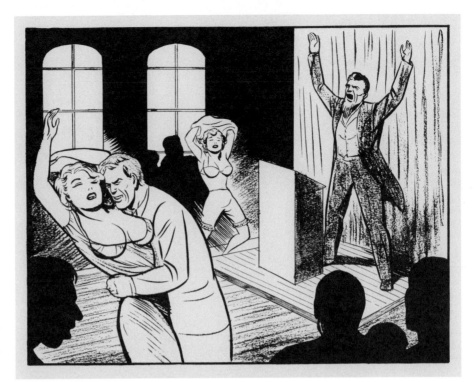

The assemblage was whipped into a frenzy by Seth's exhortations.

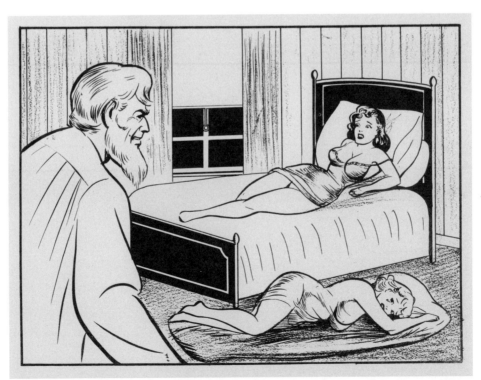

He found her timidly and fearfully waiting for him.

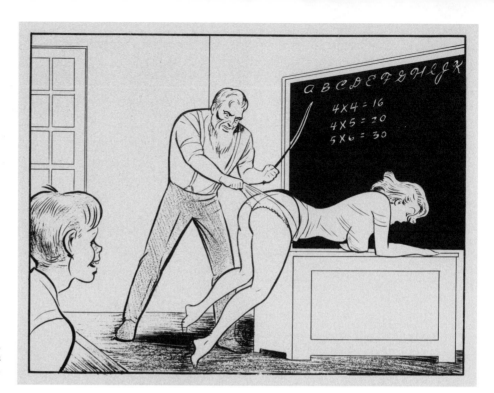

Stepping forward, he grasped the hem of Ann's panties.

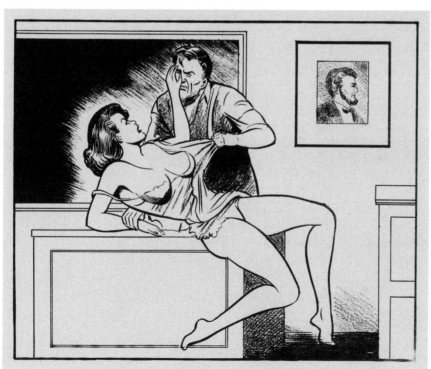

His hand seized her dress and tore it off her shoulders.

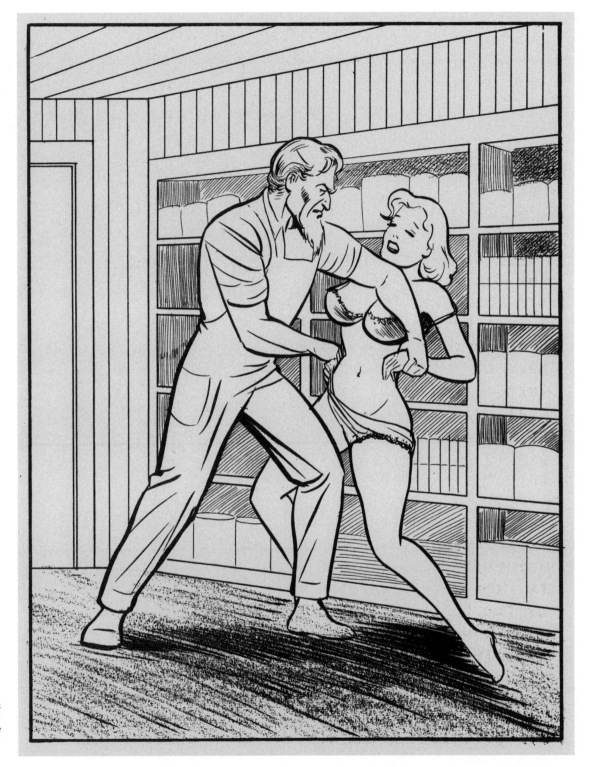

Seth seized her arm
in a crushing grip,
and brought her face
to face to him.

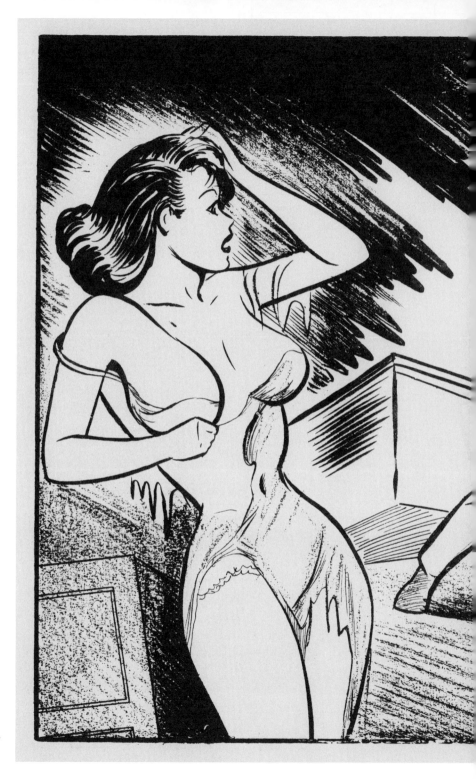

*"He's insane!
He's a beast! He
tried to—to—"*

Nights of Horror
Issue No. 14

This potboiler starts off with young Carol sitting on a riverbank with her boyfriend, Jerry, who spouts things like, "Gee Carol, it's nice here, isn't it?" Jerry doesn't go beyond a fully clothed first base when the couple is discovered by Carol's stepfather. Stepdad turns out to be a sadistic perv, who punishes his young daughter with a willow switch and forces himself on her. Carol books on a bus out of town. On the bus, she meets up with an older woman, Eleanor Wright, who is a lesbian. After seducing Carol, Wright introduces her to Ho Chin Wong, "the Oriental master of the whip." In her adventures, Carol intimately learns a hard lesson about Wright and Wong.

The back cover of this issue of *Nights of Horror* proclaims, "This is a story that will make one's blood boil at the strange torment that's inflicted on young Carol in her Ordeal of Sin." It's not clear whether the readers' blood is supposed to boil from anger or excitement—or both.

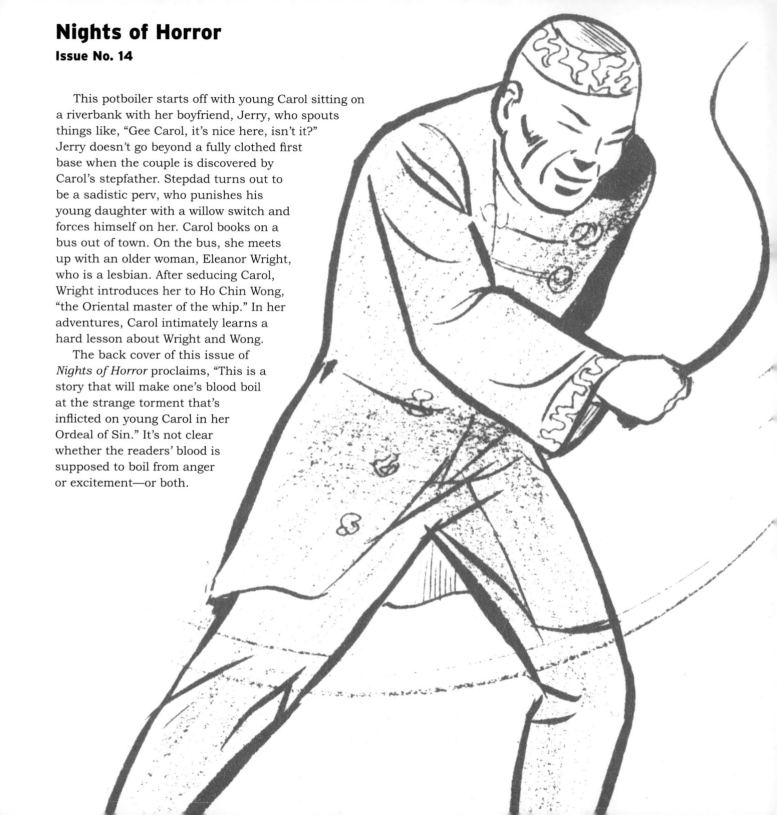

"Ordeal of Sin"

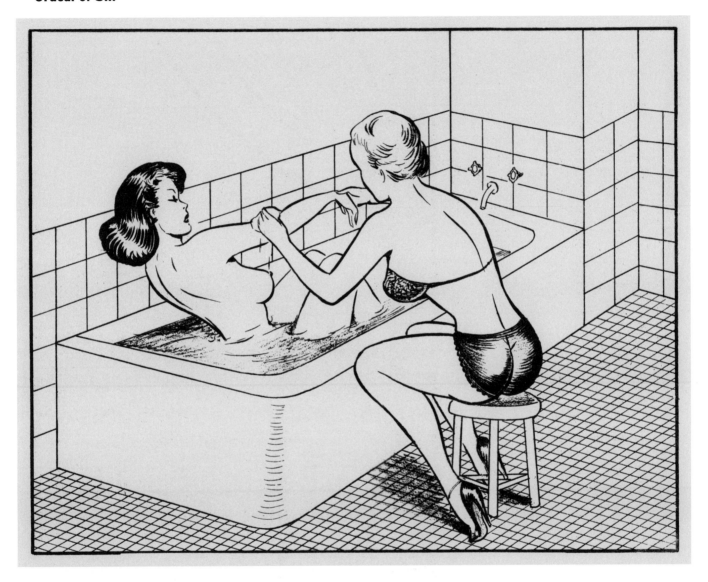

*Over Carol's feeble protests
Eleanor began to bathe the
younger girl's body.*

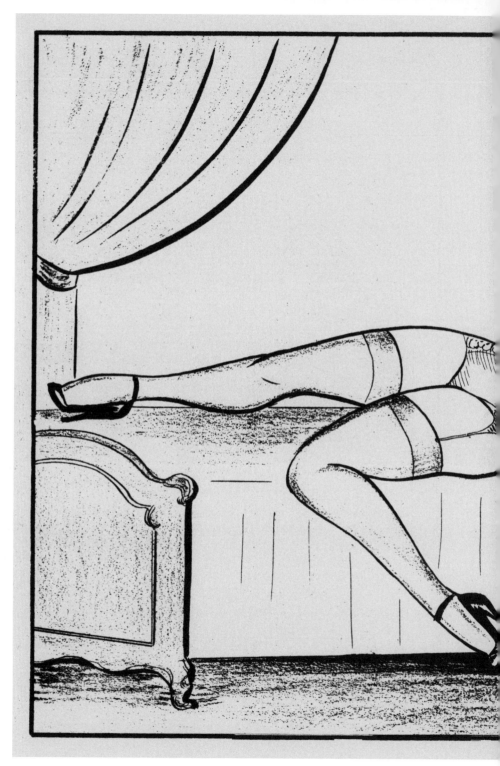

"Ooohhhhhh!"
Carol uttered a
gasping moan of
pure pleasure.

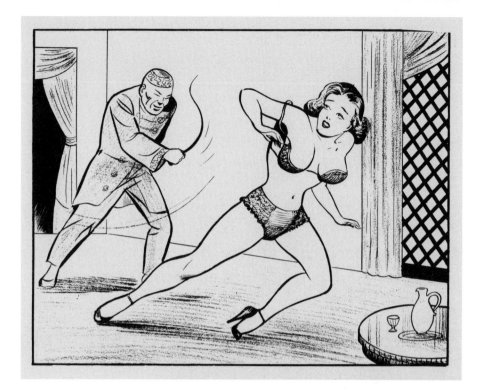

He continued to chase her around the room, flailing her shrinking body with that fearful belt.

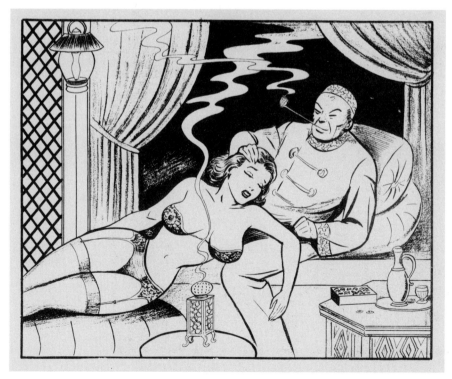

Under the influence of the drug her passions became aroused.

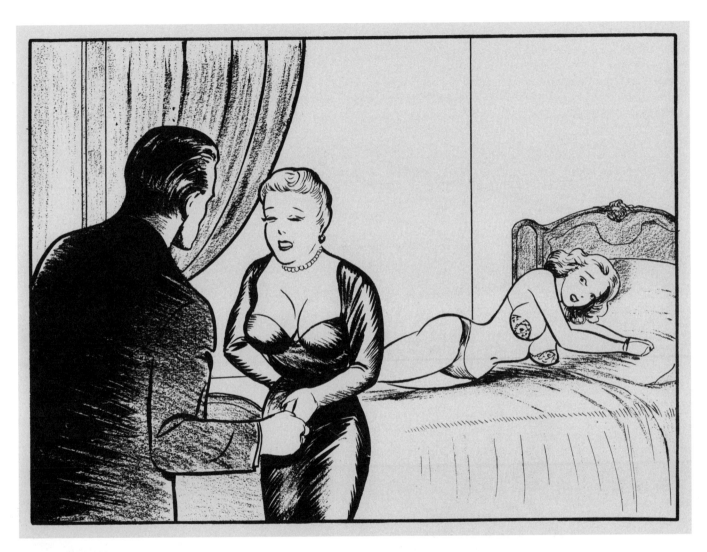

*"She's a little troublemaker whom
we've got to discipline a little."*

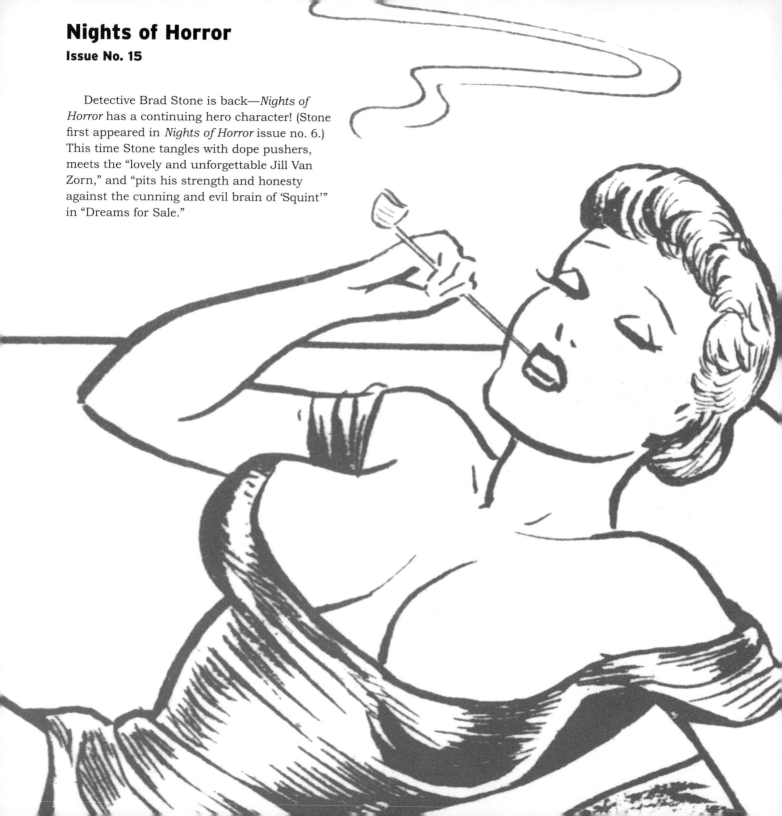

Nights of Horror
Issue No. 15

Detective Brad Stone is back—*Nights of Horror* has a continuing hero character! (Stone first appeared in *Nights of Horror* issue no. 6.) This time Stone tangles with dope pushers, meets the "lovely and unforgettable Jill Van Zorn," and "pits his strength and honesty against the cunning and evil brain of 'Squint'" in "Dreams for Sale."

"Dreams for Sale"

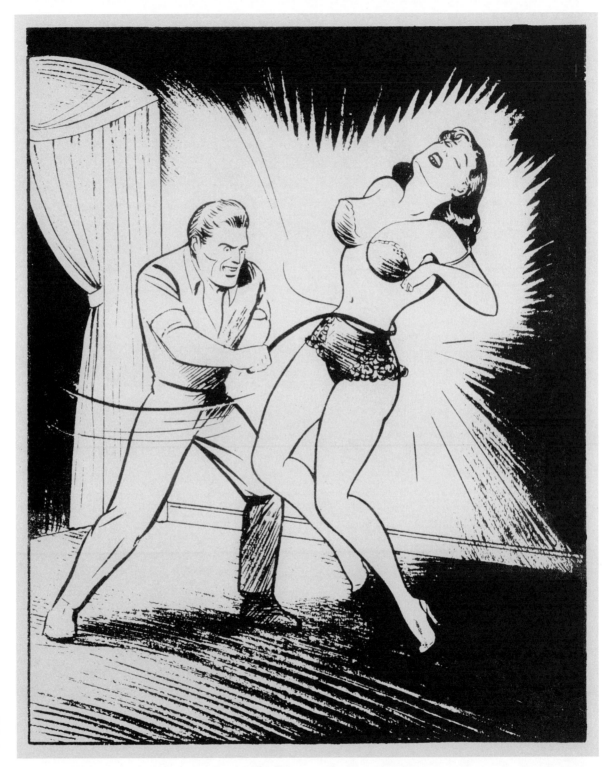

*The little man
wielded the whip
with blazing relish.*

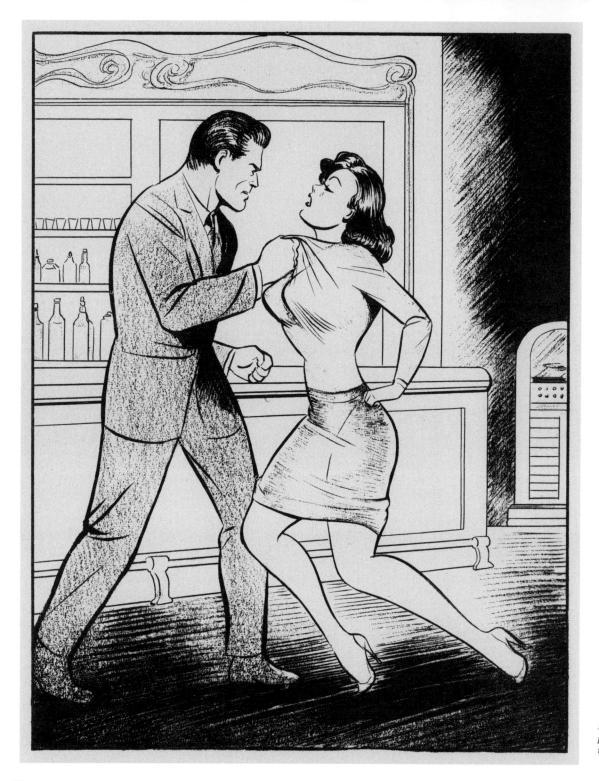

He grasped and pulled her roughly to him.

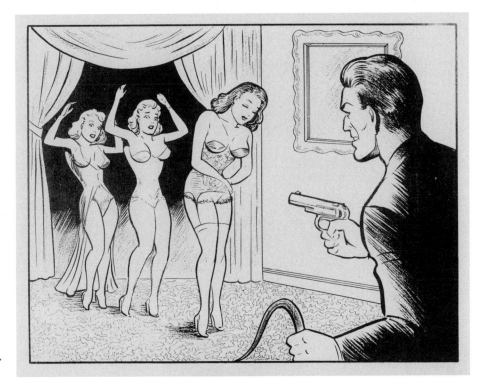

He ordered the girls to "strip down."

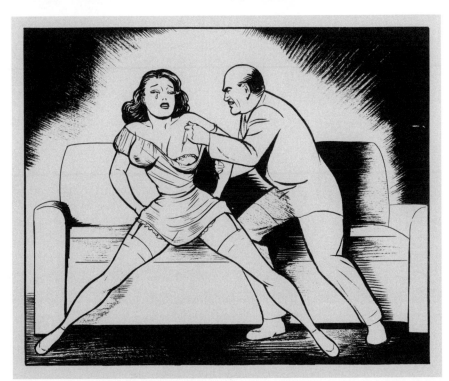

Her madness for the drug led her to forsake all shame and modesty.

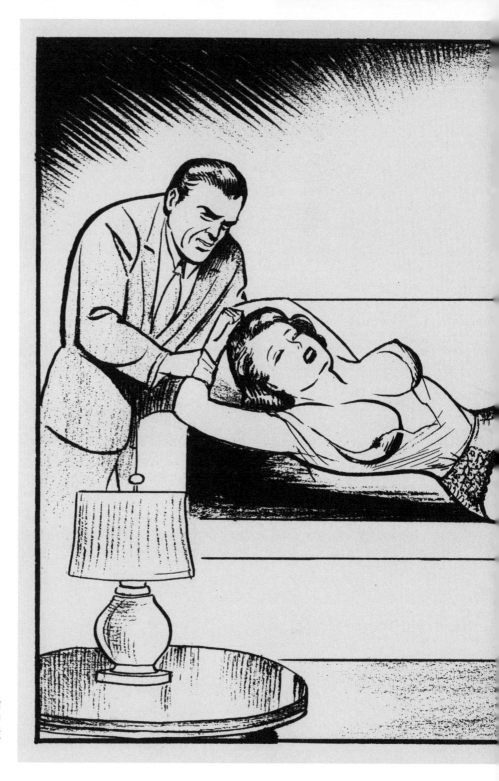

She struggled but was helpless against the both of them!

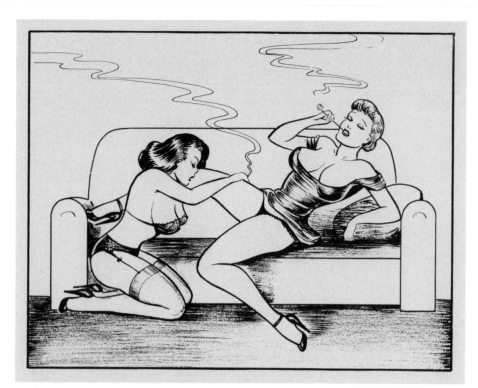

The drug stimulated their jaded appetite.

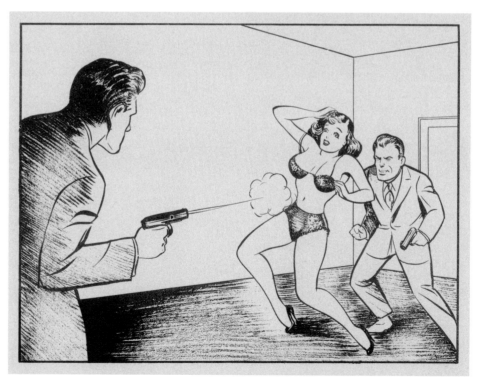

The lead messenger found a different target.

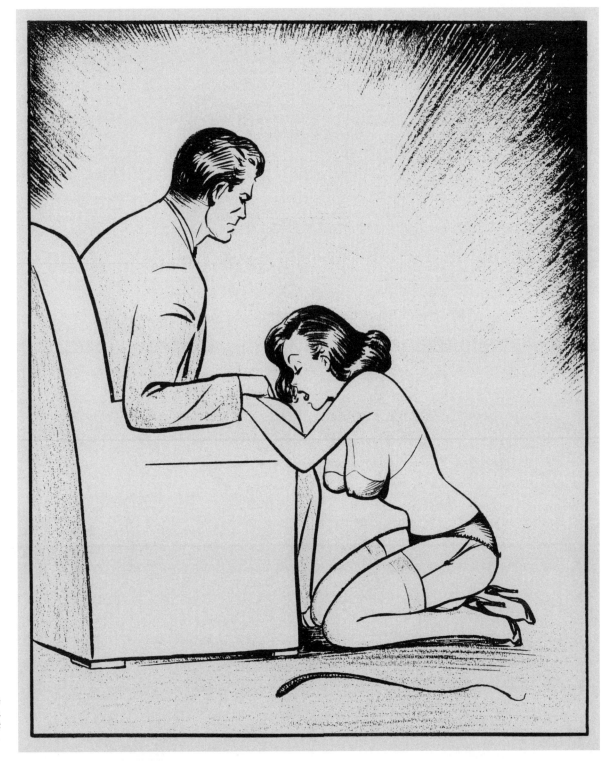

Strange desires filled his brain as she knelt before him.

Nights of Horror

Issue No. 16

A new detective hero, Duff Grimes, is introduced in the last issue of *Nights of Horror.* For "The Flesh Merchants," Joe Shuster gets to draw beautiful showgirls—a subject he was said to be well acquainted with.

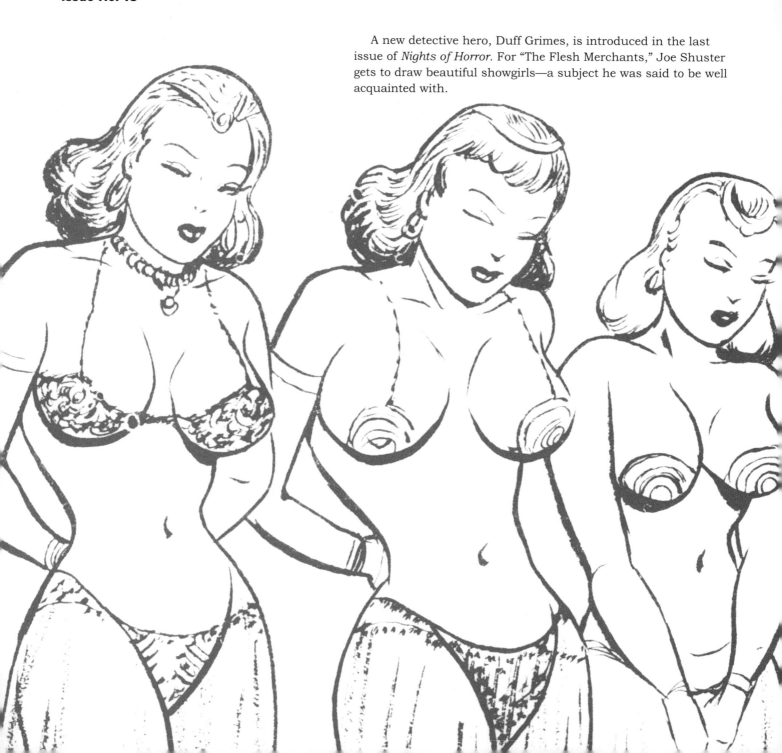

"The Flesh Merchants"

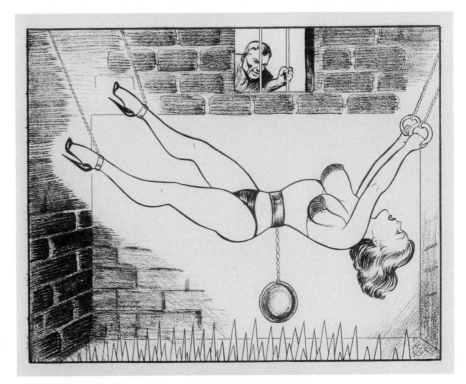

*Her muscles cried
out in agony.*

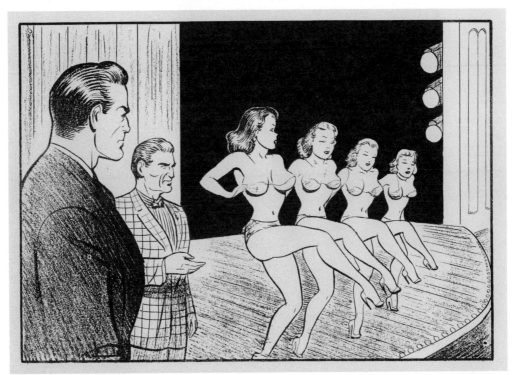

*With lusting eyes
they examined
the girls.*

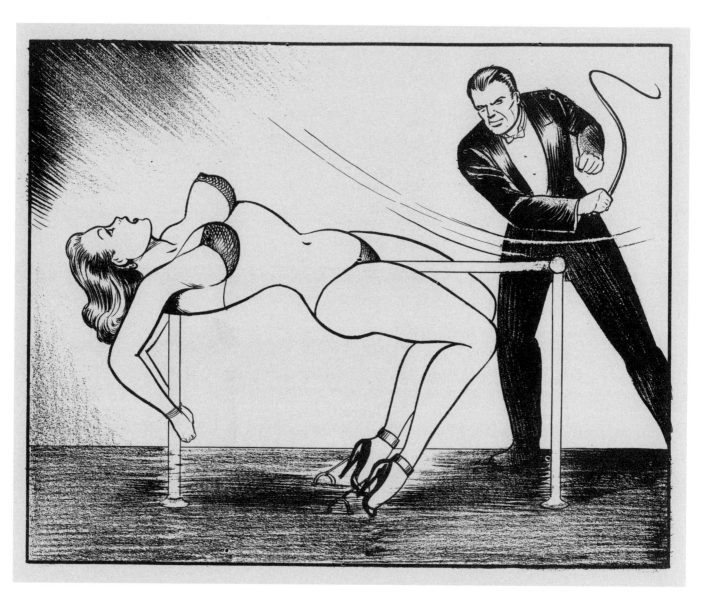

The bite of the whip felt like hot wire!

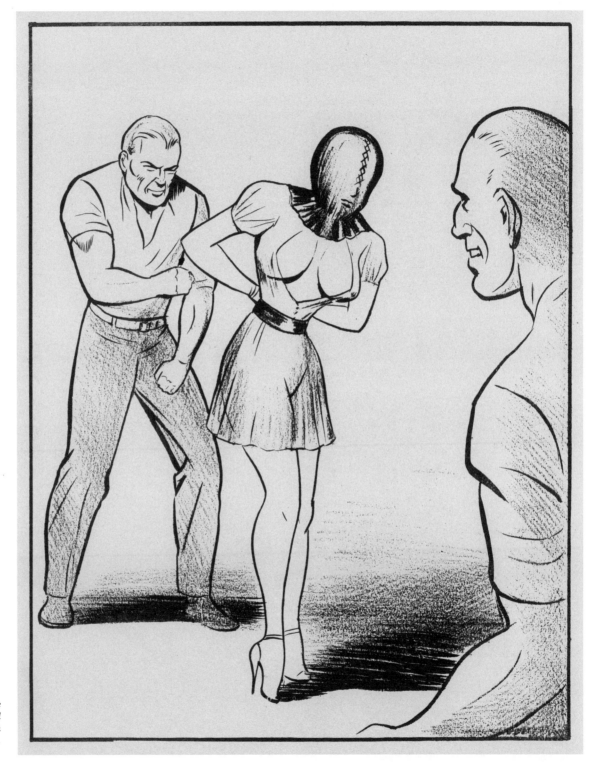

The impenetrable darkness terrified her more then anything else.

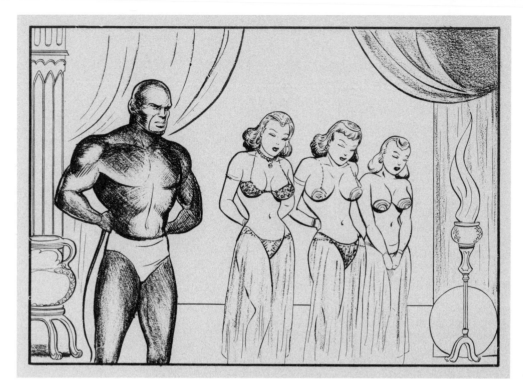

"Three beauties for sale!"

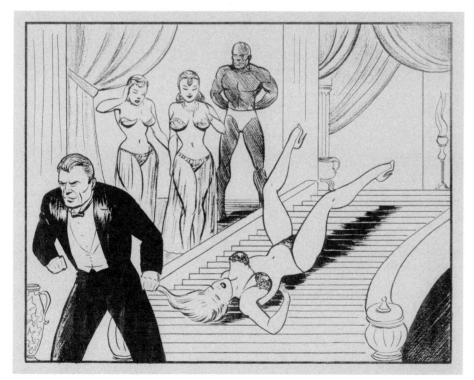

The high bidder dragged his prize down the stairs!

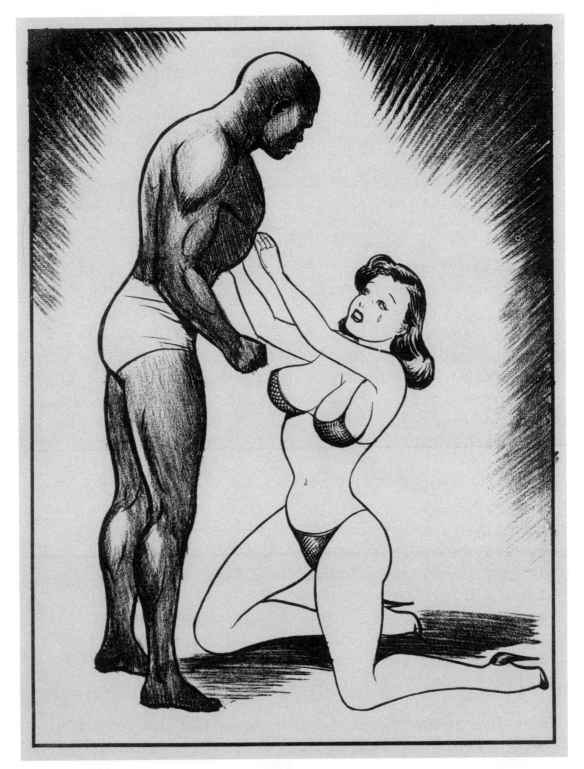

Her pleas for mercy fell on deaf ears.

Hollywood Detective

Duff Grimes, who starred in the last *Nights of Horror* (issue no. 16), is the hero of this book, too. This was probably slated to be *Nights of Horror* issue no.17, but the name simply changed to *Hollywood Detective* to protect the guilty. The sizzle copy on the back extols, "From all over the country they came—young beautiful girls seeking fame and fortune. Some find it but most don't. A few unscrupulous movie men have been luring these girls into making 'special' movies, dragging them down into shame and degradation. It is here that Duff Grimes 'HOLLYWOOD DETECTIVE' goes into action, making highly exciting and action-packed reading."

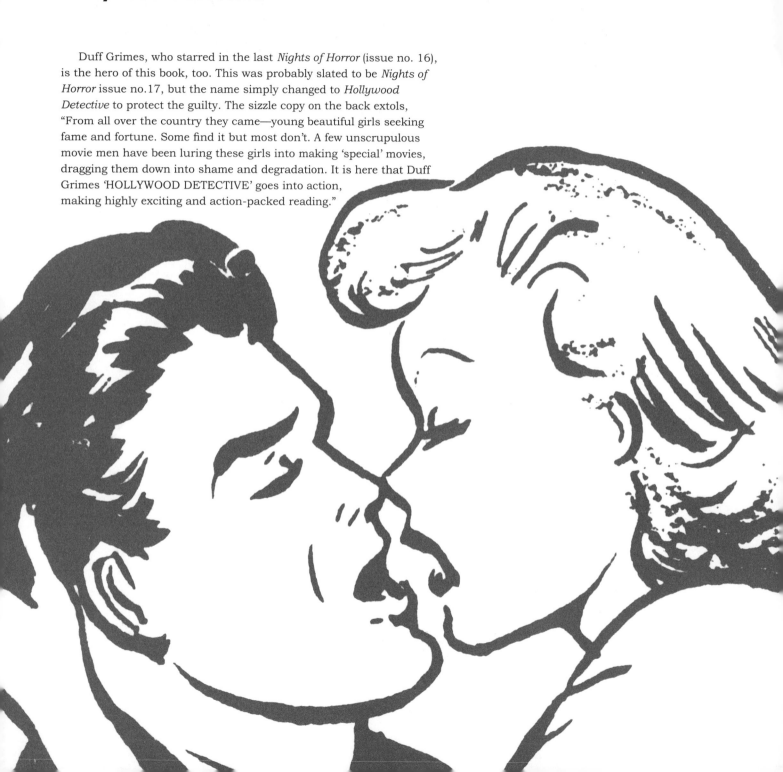

"Film Torment"

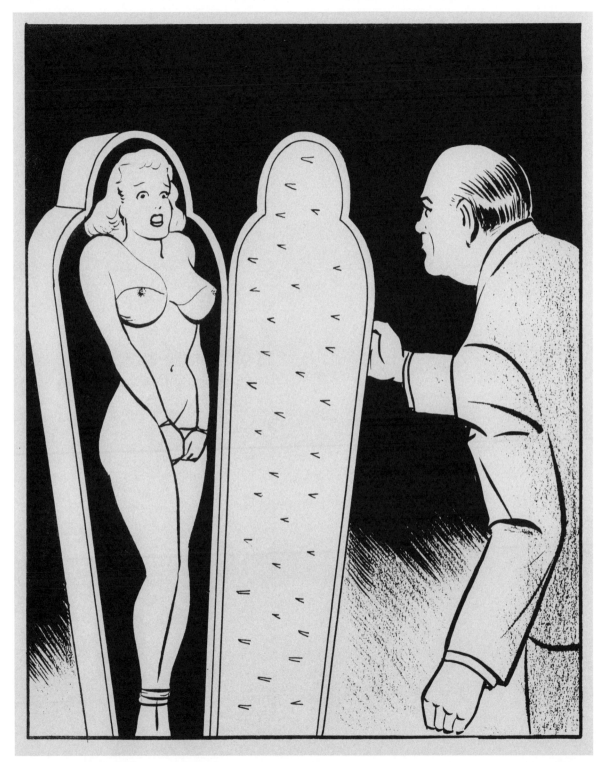

This was the iron maiden, a medieval torture device.

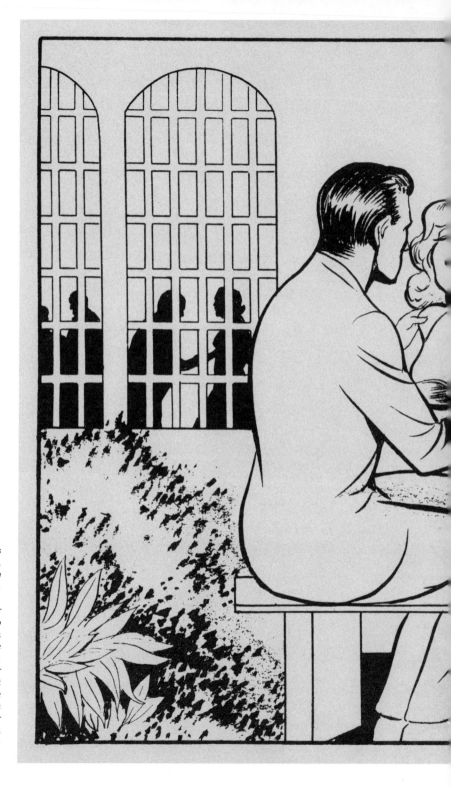

"Mmmm—this is nice," she said, leaning drunkenly against him.

(Batman's co-creator Bob Kane claimed to have dated Marilyn Monroe and that she modeled for him. Maybe Joe Shuster didn't get a date, but he sure seems to be using Marilyn as his inspiration for this picture in Hollywood Detective.)

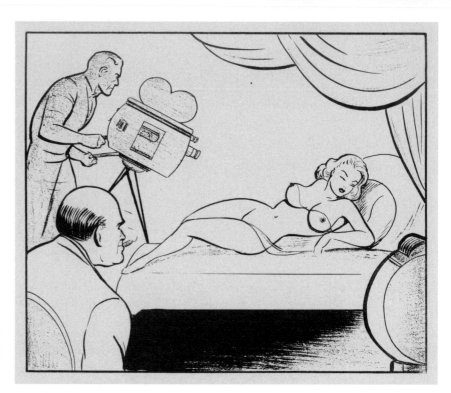

Nora assumed the first pose, her face flushing with embarrassment.

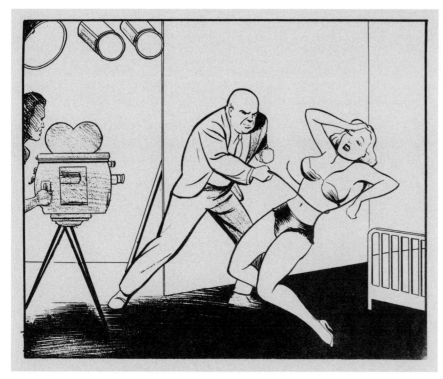

Her shrieks and cries and pleas lent added impetus to his fury.

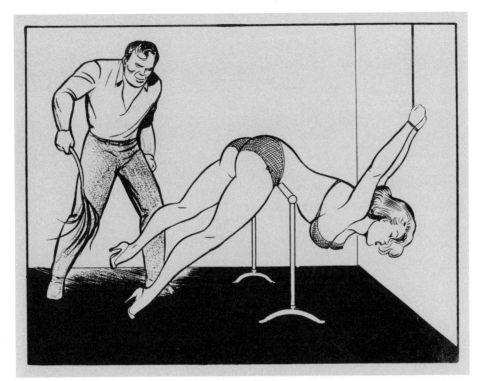

He eyed the lush beauty and his breath whistled through his teeth with eagerness.

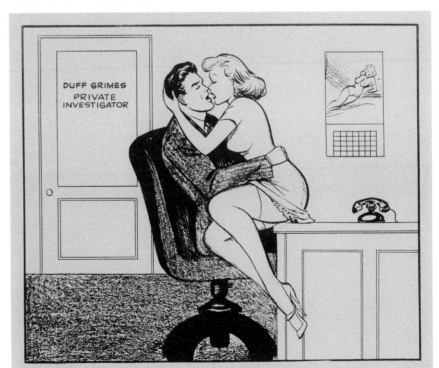

She wound her arms around his neck and pressed herself to him.

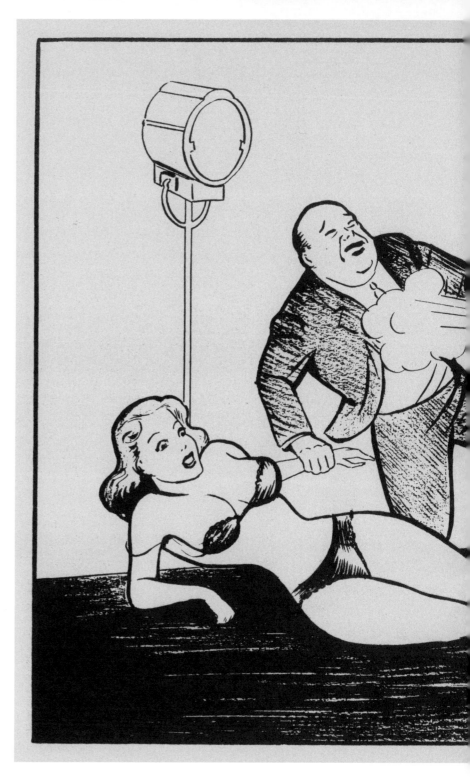

He raised the lash, but Duff fired, and Karnack fell to the floor.

Rod Rule

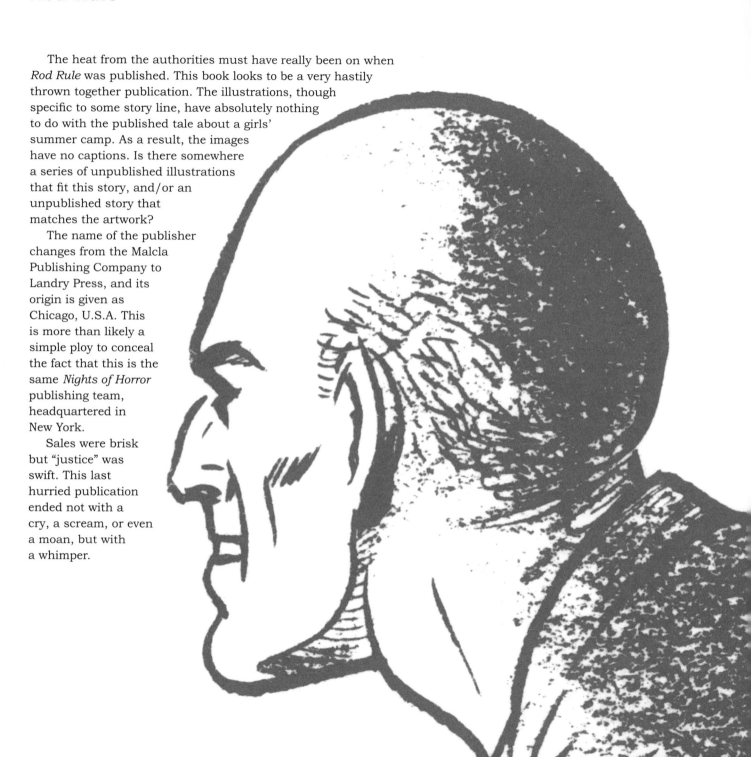

The heat from the authorities must have really been on when *Rod Rule* was published. This book looks to be a very hastily thrown together publication. The illustrations, though specific to some story line, have absolutely nothing to do with the published tale about a girls' summer camp. As a result, the images have no captions. Is there somewhere a series of unpublished illustrations that fit this story, and/or an unpublished story that matches the artwork?

The name of the publisher changes from the Malcla Publishing Company to Landry Press, and its origin is given as Chicago, U.S.A. This is more than likely a simple ploy to conceal the fact that this is the same *Nights of Horror* publishing team, headquartered in New York.

Sales were brisk but "justice" was swift. This last hurried publication ended not with a cry, a scream, or even a moan, but with a whimper.

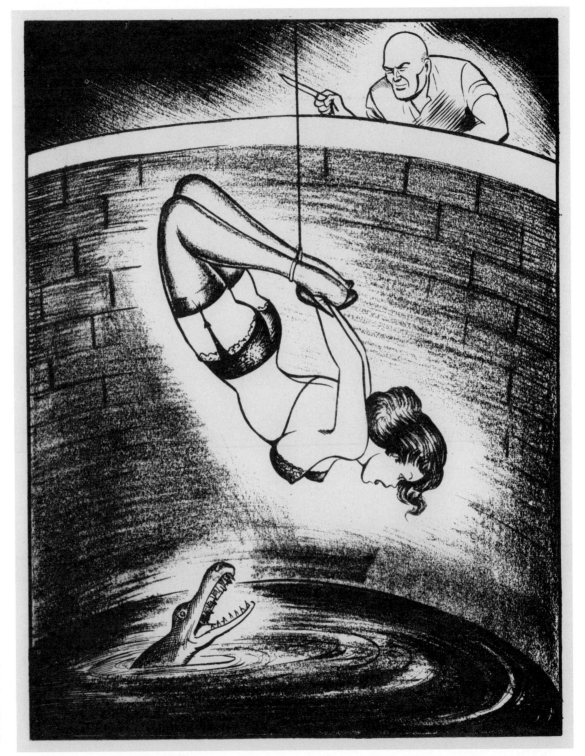

(What is fascinating about these illustrations is how closely the villain resembles Lex Luthor and the victim Lois Lane.)

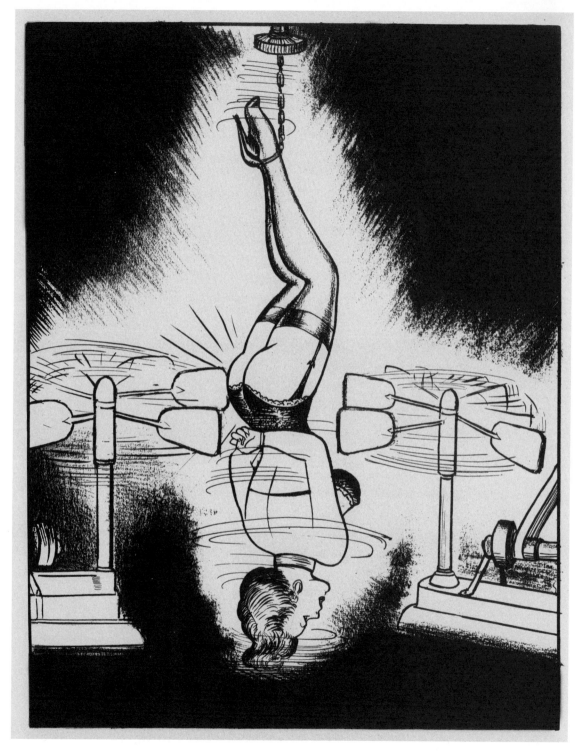

(Joe Shuster does Rube Goldberg.)

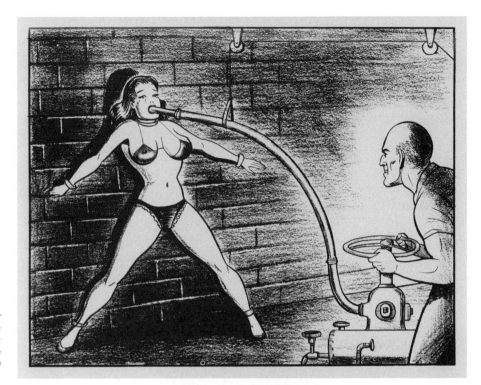

(The illustrations for Rod Rule are some of the most violent and disturbing Shuster did.)

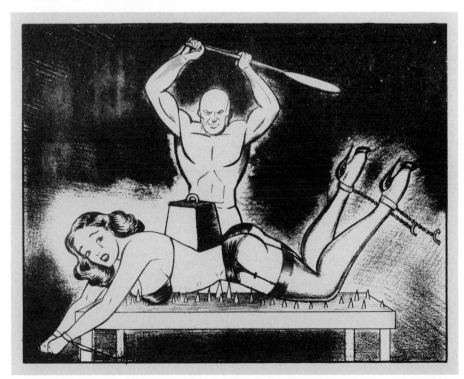

(Where is Superman when you need him?)

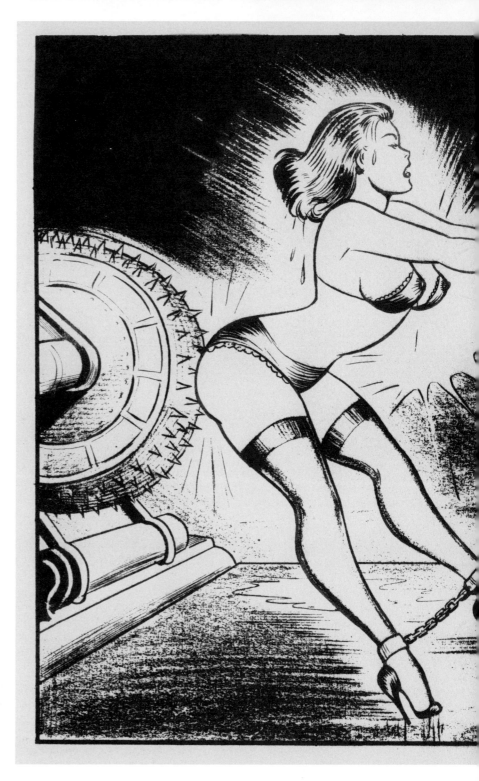

(Both Dr. Fredric Wertham and Sigmund Freud would have a lot to say about this scene.)

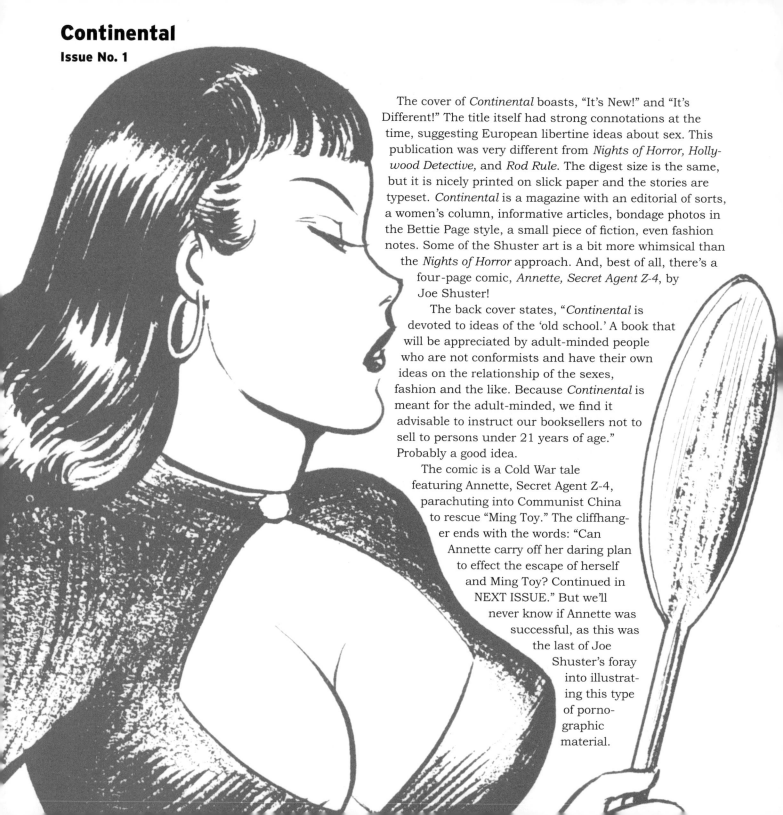

Continental

Issue No. 1

The cover of *Continental* boasts, "It's New!" and "It's Different!" The title itself had strong connotations at the time, suggesting European libertine ideas about sex. This publication was very different from *Nights of Horror, Hollywood Detective,* and *Rod Rule.* The digest size is the same, but it is nicely printed on slick paper and the stories are typeset. *Continental* is a magazine with an editorial of sorts, a women's column, informative articles, bondage photos in the Bettie Page style, a small piece of fiction, even fashion notes. Some of the Shuster art is a bit more whimsical than the *Nights of Horror* approach. And, best of all, there's a four-page comic, *Annette, Secret Agent Z-4,* by Joe Shuster!

The back cover states, "*Continental* is devoted to ideas of the 'old school.' A book that will be appreciated by adult-minded people who are not conformists and have their own ideas on the relationship of the sexes, fashion and the like. Because *Continental* is meant for the adult-minded, we find it advisable to instruct our booksellers not to sell to persons under 21 years of age." Probably a good idea.

The comic is a Cold War tale featuring Annette, Secret Agent Z-4, parachuting into Communist China to rescue "Ming Toy." The cliffhanger ends with the words: "Can Annette carry off her daring plan to effect the escape of herself and Ming Toy? Continued in NEXT ISSUE." But we'll never know if Annette was successful, as this was the last of Joe Shuster's foray into illustrating this type of pornographic material.

"Old Fashioned"

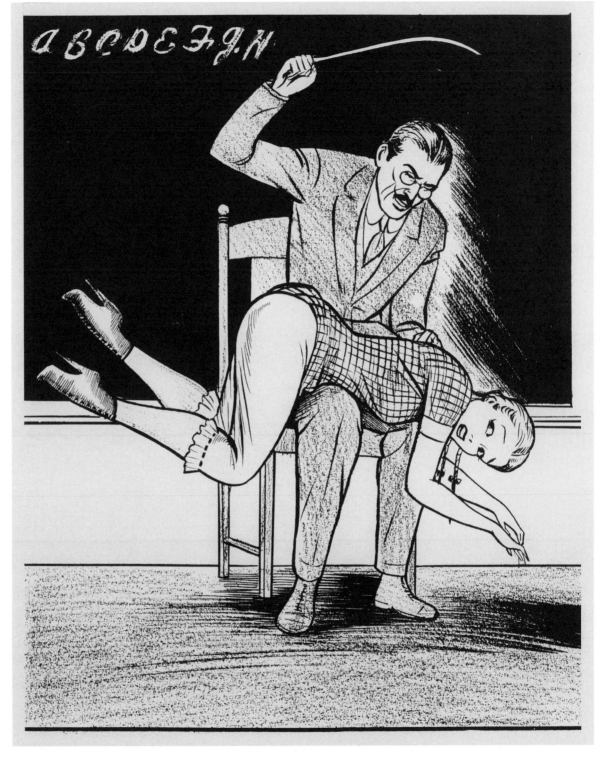

Nowadays, we hear much about progressive education. To administer a sound licking or paddling to unruly children is not the thing to do. Psychology is to be used, talk and reason with the child, but not, no never, physical punishment. We have only to read our newspapers today to get the answer to the question of whether this modern method is working out or not. No matter what newspaper you read, feature stories of juvenile delinquents are prominent.

(Contrary to Dr. Fredric Wertham's belief, "Old Fashioned" espouses that juvenile delinquency isn't caused by comic books and pornography, but by a lack of good spankings administered by teachers.)

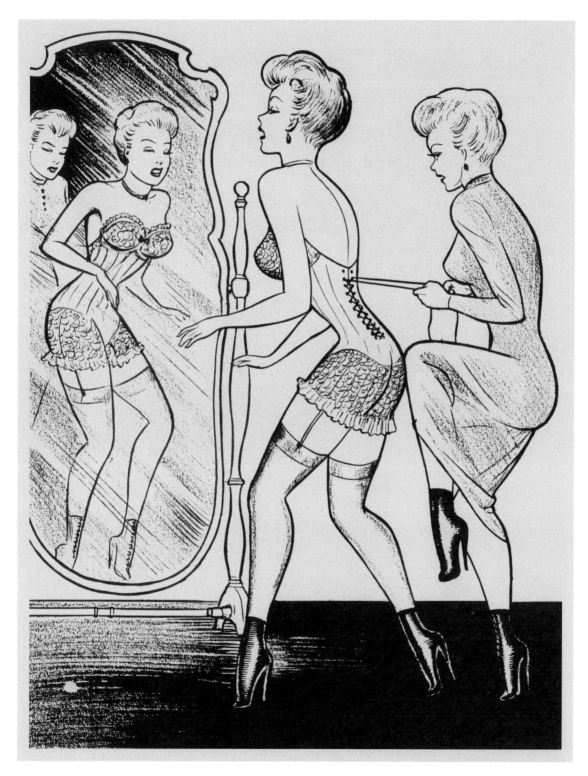

Picture a young,
beautiful girl of 18
who has been
disrespectful to her
parents . . . A tight
corset binds her
waist trimly . . .
Here then is
discipline with
useful purpose and
accomplishment.

"Education?"

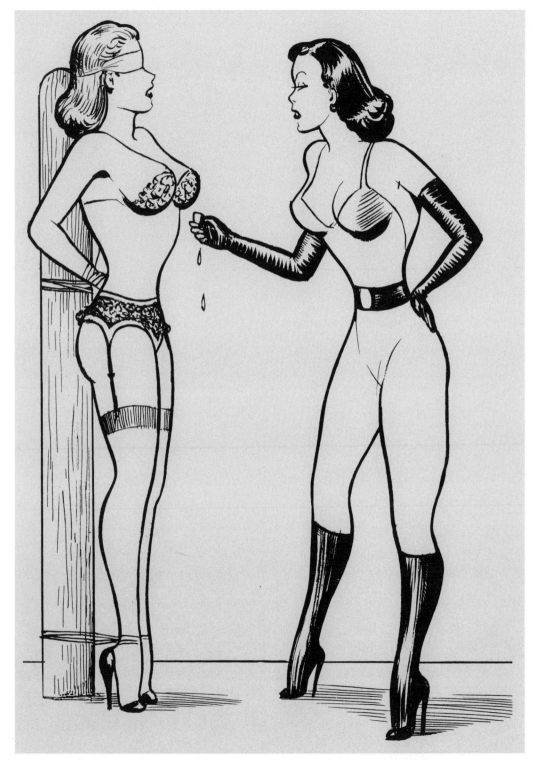

"And now, girls," Cleo continued, "for the second part of your initiation tonight we're going to put the sorority initials on you so that you will always be able to prove to one another that you are real members of the group."

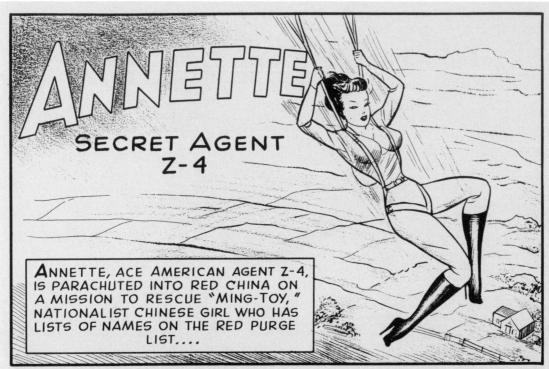

ANNETTE, ACE AMERICAN AGENT Z-4, IS PARACHUTED INTO RED CHINA ON A MISSION TO RESCUE "MING-TOY," NATIONALIST CHINESE GIRL WHO HAS LISTS OF NAMES ON THE RED PURGE LIST....

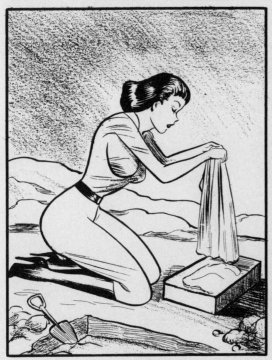

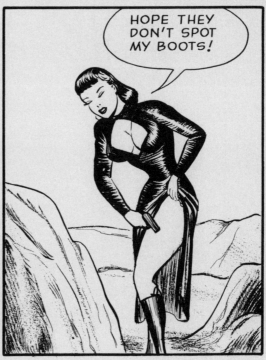

HOPE THEY DON'T SPOT MY BOOTS!

THE BEASTS! LOOK WHAT THEY'RE DOING TO MING TOY!

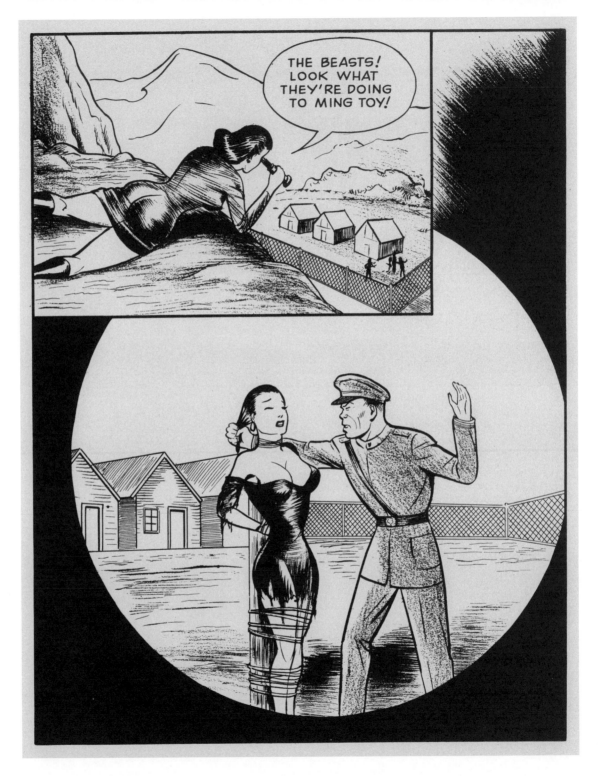

TAKE HER BACK TO HER CELL-- WE'LL MAKE HER GIVE US THE LIST YET!
YES, MAJOR CHEN!
IT'S LUCKY I CAN READ LIPS-- MAJOR CHEN WILL RECEIVE A VISITOR TONIGHT!
MAJOR CHEN IS EXPECTING ME!

HERE IS THE GIRL YOU SENT FOR, COMRADE MAJOR...
I DIDN'T SEND FOR YOU-- BUT NOW THAT YOU'RE HERE...
COMRADE, PLEASE!
KEEP YOUR EYES CLOSED AND I'LL GIVE YOU THAT SURPRISE IN A MOMENT...
CAN ANNETTE CARRY OFF HER DARING PLAN TO EFFECT THE ESCAPE OF HERSELF AND MING TOY? CONTINUED IN NEXT ISSUE.

The End

In "Nights Of Horror" we have endeavored to bring to you stories spiced and illustrated in a way we know you will enjoy.

Tales of strange loves, spicy mystery & Adventure will be found in "Nights Of Horror".

If you enjoy this volume, ask your book seller for more issues of "Nights Of Horror".

———————————

ABOVE: *The back cover copy from* Nights of Horror.